TEENAGERS & TODDLERS
ARE TRYING TO KILL ME!

Also by Susan Konig

Why Animals Sleep So Close to the Road (and Other Lies I Tell My Children)
I Wear the Maternity Pants in This Family

Teenagers & Toddlers Are Trying to Kill Me!

Based on a true story

Susan Konig

Willow Street Press New York

Some of the essays in this book previously appeared in some form in the
following publications:
Catholic Digest and *National Review* Online.

ISBN: 0989538109
ISBN 13: 978-0-989-53810-7

Printed in the United States of America
FIRST EDITION

Cover illustration/design: Megan Montague Cash

For my children who inspired this book.

And for my husband who is largely responsible for our having all these kids.

ACKNOWLEDGEMENTS

Many thanks to my husband and our kids for encouraging me to "finish the book already!"

Thanks to my editors, Traci Neal at *Catholic Digest* and Kathryn Jean Lopez at National Review Online, for giving me space.

To Don Odom for his publishing wisdom.

For my mom, who survived my childhood with grace.

And in memory of two JBs -- my dad and my best friend.

CONTENTS

PROLOGUE: ALONE TOGETHER? NOT LIKELY!

I don't go out much. Angelina Jolie I'm not. I don't travel the globe walking the red carpet with Brad Pitt and accumulating tattoos. I am home with two moody teenagers, one mischievous tween, one sticky toddler, a cranky spouse, a shedding dog, a snoring cat, a standoffish turtle and two beady-eyed goldfish. When I go out, it's a major occurrence – rare, like a Sasquatch sighting [see epilogue for details on Sasquatch sightings].

When I do manage to escape, it takes about three minutes before they find me, before my phone rings -- so either I am still driving or I am just starting down the first aisle of the grocery store (yes, I really go wild when I get away from the family). My phone lights up and vibrates. I can't ignore the texts – it could be an emergency. "A large bookshelf has fallen on dad -- what do we do?"

But it's never about my husband trapped under furniture. Instead, I get this:

"Mom, where r u?"

"Mom, when r u coming home?"

"Bring food."

"Mom, when you come home, bring food – and when r u coming home?"

Of course, these same frantically texting kids seem perfectly fine when I get home – and the teenagers ignore me. Oddly they all vanish completely when they see me coming up the walkway with twenty bags of groceries to put away. They're hungry, but not that hungry.

And it doesn't matter if Dad is home, too. It's Mom that gets the calls. Once, I got a call from our Teenage Son asking, "Hey, Mom. So say I broke my glasses. Would that be something that I could just go to the glasses store and they could fix?"

I took a breath. "What happened?"

"Nothing. I'm just wondering how that would work."

"Are your glasses broken?"

"Well, I was playing basketball and they kinda got stepped on…twice."

We'd bought him expensive sports goggles. They were safely at home in his top drawer while some kid's size 14 Air Jordans were squashing his wire frames into the asphalt of the town basketball court.

"Is Dad home?"

"Yeah, but I think he's resting…"

Uh-huh.

"Could you please gently rouse your dad from his beauty nap and have him get the heck over to the eyeglass store before they close?"

One winter weekend, a bunch of high school boys came over to play touch football with our Teenage Son, the one with the broken glasses. I made hot dogs for everyone, brought a case of water and a box of cookies out to the porch. Then I had some errands to run.

When I left, our Toddler was standing on top of a pile of snow in our front yard waving a broom and yelling at the boys playing in the street. I gave our Teenage Son the standard instructions: "Watch your brother, and don't let him in the road, Dad's right inside."

I did a quick spin through the dry cleaners, ATM, and drug store. When I returned, twenty minutes later, our Toddler was still standing on top of the icy mounds yelling but now, instead of sweat pants, he had inexplicably changed into a bathing suit. In February.

I got out of the car. "Why is he wearing a bathing suit?"

"I dunno," came the classic teenage reply.

I went inside. I asked my husband, "Why is your son wearing a bathing suit in 40 degree weather?"

"Which son?"

My five-year-old explained that his sweats got a little wet and dirty playing in the old snow and he couldn't find another pair of pants so he just put on his swimsuit. Seemed logical to him. A bathing suit is supposed to get wet -- so it's the perfect thing to wear in the snow in February.

Until spring, I may just try to stick very close to home.

The thing about having a lot of kids is that, eventually, they get older and parents get their lives back. Right? Well, at least that's what I hear. At one point, my husband and I had three children under five and three car seats in our minivan -- we were practically running a daycare center on wheels. But time passed and the first two went to school and then came that glorious day when the third and youngest child got on the school bus to kindergarten.

All three in school – full days! We made it! Light, meet tunnel!

I went inside, fixed myself a relaxing cup of tea – then I ran to the bathroom and threw up.

I was pregnant again. At age 43. Back to babies, diapers, strollers, the whole megillah.

Still, time continued to pass and, with sunshine, vitamin D and fortified milk, the children continued to grow. Even the baby. So now, elderly and exhausted, we are in a new phase where the older kids are teenagers, the middle son is still in the middle, and the new baby is now a toddler. But, and here's the good part: now that the older children are teenagers, my husband and I can go out. We can legally leave the house and try to do what we used to do long, long ago. Go on dates (I should clarify: with each other).

But it has been so long. What if it's changed? What's out there? Do restaurants still serve food? Or do they just give you a food pill and you return to your flying car? Yes, it has been that long.

My husband is always telling me that we need some "alone time." He wants to have a quiet, romantic dinner. Actually, I want to have a quiet, romantic dinner. He'd settle for a conversation that's not punctuated with interruptions and fights, other than those generated by him or me.

"Alone time" is science fiction in a house as crowded as ours – the kids, the pets…did I mention we have the occasional lizard? (But no partridge in a pear tree. If there was one, it was eaten by the lizard.) Most of all there is no peace since the teenagers and toddlers are convinced that Copernicus was wrong – the Earth doesn't revolve around the sun. It revolves around them!

"I will kill whoever ate my pudding!"

"There's a giant spider in the bathtub!"

"Where's the pencil sharpener? I promise not to stab anyone this time!"

My husband thinks he's the king of the castle, but he is a lonely monarch whose reign goes largely unnoticed. It's not that the Emperor has no clothes -- clothes he's got. It's just that no one's paying attention; there's too much going on. Even when my long-suffering husband and I sneak a quick embrace in the kitchen, the dog jumps on him. We're not sure why but that dog does not want us to have a moment. Is the dog jealous? Anti-Semitic? We can't figure it out.

He doesn't think this is as funny as I think it is. (My husband, that is, not the dog.) It's not that I don't want to be alone with him. It's just such a foreign concept at this point. And alone we never really are.

But the new plan is that we will go out at least once a week (translation: every third or fifth month) and the teenagers will watch the toddlers. We will sneak out for an hour, leaving them with everything they need: a refrigerator full of food, a box of pizza, a TV, a Netflix subscription, and multiple rooms to get away from each other. What could possibly go wrong?

Before the waitress can bring us a basket of flab-inducing bread, the calls and texts begin anew.

"Your son is trying to stab me with a fork!"

"Mom, didn't you say I could stay up?"

"Tell them you left me in charge...no one is listening to me!"

"She called me stupid!"

"Hope you and dad are having a nice date. BTW did you put any money in my debit account?? Xo :)"

"OK, now non-stop screaming. The neighbors had to come over. Complete meltdown..."

I text back: "SEPARATE!!!!!!!" All caps, lots of exclamation points, that's how moms yell in text.

Now I'm in a foul mood. Am I mad at the kids? Maybe. But they're not sitting across from me – my husband is. So now I'm mad at him. Why? How come I'm the one getting the play-by-play of the carnage? Look at him -- he just sits there eating bread. I haven't had one bite. Him they don't text. "That's because they know they can negotiate with you," he says, shoving more bread into his face.

From now on, if we go out for a romantic dinner, it's probably easier just to bring the kids with us. After all, everyone's got to eat.

"Mom, how long is this gonna take? I want to hang out with my friends."

"No chicken fingers? What am I supposed to eat?"

"Mommy, I have to poop."

At least they aren't constantly texting me during the meal. I look at my husband as I take the Toddler to the restroom. "Meet me at the retirement home in twenty years. We'll have a nice quiet dinner. Bring your teeth!"

SUPERMODEL'S BREASTFEEDING LAW A BIG BUST

When our Teenage Daughter was born and we became first time parents, my husband and I kept a "feeding notebook" for weeks. I had received breast feeding instruction in the hospital from the diehard lactation specialists of the La Leche League (or, as my husband mysteriously calls them, "the Café Con Leche Society.") They didn't want me giving my baby any formula at all. "No formula!" they said. They were very adamant about it. There might have been some clicking of heels, too. I'm not sure, I was a little woozy.

Aggressive as they were and as worn down as I was, I waited until they left, then made sure that there was plenty of formula for the baby. I was sleeping a lot following an emergency C-section so I was very happy to have other humans available to give her a bottle. Over the next few days, the baby and I worked it out so I could breast feed, too. It wasn't an easy experience, but it was a beautiful one.

When we brought her home, we were like most first-time parents: completely terrified we might do something wrong and somehow "break" the baby! So we kept copious notes of everything going into the baby (not so much on what was coming out). Here are actual notes from our actual note-taking:

Midnight: four ounces bottle. Spit up.

12:20 AM: Breastfed 20 minutes. Spit up.

1:00 AM: Breastfed 20 minutes. Spit up.

2:20 AM: Bottle four ounces.

3:00 AM: Breastfed 45 minutes. Spit up a lot.

5:00 AM: Breastfed 2 hours.

For similar exercises in rational writing, see Jack Nicholson in *The Shining*.

This schedule was punctuated by exhaustion and insanity and with me yelling helpful things at my husband like, "I'M JUST TRYING TO FEED MY BABY!!!!!" (Note the all caps and exclamation points -- and this was before texting.)

We brought the week-old baby and the notebook into our first pediatrician appointment.

"'Breastfed 2 hours!?' What the heck are you doing?"

"We have no idea!"

He put us on a schedule and things got better. After about 2 months, I stopped breastfeeding her which was also painful as the milk continued to build up. If you've ever had a part of your body completely filled with a beverage and were counting on someone who has only been alive for eight weeks to alleviate, then you know what I'm talking about. We finally tapered off, and she went straight for the bottle. So did I.

Two years later, when her brother was born weighing twelve pounds one ounce (Yes, not a typo! For a reference point on how our 12 pound bouncing boy compared to the other babies in the maternity ward, think of Godzilla and the citizens of Tokyo), I declined the breastfeeding option as I was terrified by potential production quotas and wanted as many people as possible to be able to help me nourish the bruiser. I didn't breastfeed the next two boys because I didn't want to play favorites.

Which brings me, naturally enough, to Supermodel Gisele Bundchen. She once proposed that an international law be passed mandating all babies, worldwide, be breastfed for the first six months. Before this decree, Miss Bundchen was primarily known for being paid to wear her underwear in public.

The oft-photographed lingerie model made the big pronouncement after having her own baby: "I think there should be a worldwide law that mothers breastfeed their babies for six months."

Supermodel/international breast feeding expert Gisele Bundchen quickly clarified on her Web site: "I am not here to judge."

Along with the proposed mandatory nursing law, Supermodel/international breast feeding expert/NFL trash talker Gisele Bundchen also chimed in on the subject of pregnancy weight gain, "I think a lot of people get pregnant and decide they can turn into garbage disposals."

Hey, as someone who raised the stock of Ben & Jerry, gaining 185 pounds over four pregnancies, I resent that remark. Ice cream is not garbage.

If she's not here to judge, I would hate to be around when Supermodel Gisele Bundchen is in a judgmental mood.

But what do I have to worry about? Supermodel Gisele Bundchen and I clearly do not have a lot in common.

- Supermodel Gisele Bundchen practiced kung fu while pregnant.
- I ordered moo shu pork while pregnant.
- Supermodel Gisele Bundchen meditated intensely while giving birth.
- I medicated heavily while giving birth.
- Supermodel Gisele Bundchen weighs nine stone (or 126 pounds).
- I weighed nine stone – (in ninth grade).
- Supermodel Gisele Bundchen said, "I wasn't expecting someone else to get the baby out of me."
- I not only expected someone else to get all my babies out of me, I was counting on it. My first birth was an emergency C-section followed by three scheduled procedures. Each time I yelled, "Get it out! Get it out!" I would have let Supermodel Gisele Bundchen get it out.
- According to Supermodel Gisele Bundchen, her eight hours of labor "didn't hurt in the slightest."
- My fourteen hours of labor hurt a lot, followed by surgery which hurt a lot, segueing into recovery which also hurt a lot.

It's not that supermodels don't have a lot to offer.
- I would take skin advice from Cindy Crawford.
- I'd listen to yoga tips from Christy Turlington.
- I would let Christie Brinkley recommend a good divorce lawyer.

But breastfeeding advice (or mandatory international laws) from a woman who's known for two things: her underwear and cursing out her husband's teammates? Hey Gisele! Keep your hands off my breasts!

But I'm not here to judge.

UNPARALLELED PARKING

The day our Teenage Daughter turned sixteen, we went to the Department of Motor Vehicles to apply for her learner's permit. Our studious teen studied the book of road rules, took the online practice test, and was ready.

She sat for the written test and was told she passed. I was called over to pay the permit fee (of course) and I asked how my daughter did. "She got 100% -- the smarty," the woman behind the counter said.

I was proud. Since we live in the rural backwoods (well… the suburbs, 45 minutes from Broadway), getting a driver's license is much more important to my kids than it was to me. When I turned sixteen, I lived in Manhattan – the only people who owned cars were cab drivers. We only needed driver's licenses when we turned eighteen so we could go dancing at discos. Yes, discos. I was eighteen a long time ago.

So I took drivers' education. My instructor Mr. Sklar must have had some sort of Dalai Lama-like inner peace to work with a car full of teenagers at dusk in winter in Manhattan during rush hour. Either that or he was heavily medicated. He had a dual brake and a dual steering wheel. This (in addition to medication) must have contributed to his calm in the face of terror.

I did well under Mr. Sklar's watchful eye but failed parallel parking on the day of my road test. I failed parallel parking epically. Oh, I parallel parked all right – it just took me 17 moves. But I had an excuse. I stepped into a freezing puddle just when it was my turn and couldn't feel my foot. Who can parallel park with a frozen foot? My examiner was unmoved by my plight.

I abandoned my quest for an official license until I was shamed into getting one in college. See, using a passport as proof of age is uncool. I called the AAAA Driving School. Surprisingly, they were the second school in the phone book. First I called AAAAA Driving School, but their line was busy. I took a couple of lessons and passed my test. By the way, I am now a master parallel parker. I can parallel park a 1973 Dodge Coronet in one move.

But after a few driving lessons with me, my daughter has already learned some important lessons:

- When going into a turn, try not to accelerate.
- There are two methods for applying the brakes. 1) Gently ease your foot down on the brake in a gradual but firm manner. 2) Abruptly slam both feet down on brake pedal while clenching steering wheel and teeth. The first method is generally advisable.
- While the Amazing Kreskin can in fact read your mind, it is rare that he is actually in the car behind you so use your turn signals to help other drivers who are not mind readers.

- No texting while listening to your iPod while driving.
- No listening to your iPod while making cell phone calls while driving.
- No doing anything but driving while driving.

I told her, "Remember, always be super alert and aware of your surroundings."

"Like when you crashed the minivan into the Subaru in our own driveway?" she asks.

"Yes dear."

"Or when dad hit the fence backing up and tore the front fender completely off?"

"Uh-huh."

"Or when you hit the neighbor's car because she parked in your blind spot?

"Shut up and drive, honey."

CAN YOU HEAR ME NOW?

I was in my basement attempting to make a dent in the endless mountain of laundry that is a constant threat to our sanity and property values when our Teenage Son barreled in yelling, "Where's my phone? Has anyone seen my phone?" Grabbing a pair of his cargo pants from the washer, I realized they felt strangely heavy. Phone found.

I should have checked his pockets. But with the volume of laundry generated by four kids, I don't check -- I just shovel. Sometimes this system works in my favor because the dryer can yield fluffy, clean dollar bills. And who keeps the laundered money? The person who does the wash (and the Mob).

This particular cell phone had already been submerged in a swimming pool, run through the washer, and left outside on the back porch in the rain. This was the Michael Phelps of cell phones.

After the pool incident, I discovered the secret of saving a swamped phone. A bowl of rice -- uncooked, white rice. Uncle Ben's will do.

Many moms already know this trick because, picking up from the pool party, my son handed me a plastic storage container of rice. The host mom had learned, perhaps by virtue of having teenagers and a pool, the high carbohydrate technique for absorbing water out of phones.

And you know what? It works. The rice absorbs the water and the phone regains its function, though not without idiosyncrasies. My son complained that the keys don't always press correctly for texting.

"Can I call you?" I ask.

"Yes."

"Can you call me?"

"Yes."

"Then we're good."

Which is why I got phones for my kids in the first place. So I can keep tabs on them at all times!

The catch is getting the youngsters to actually bring their phones with them and make sure they are working. I am constantly reminding them:

"Keep it charged!"

"Keep it with you!"

"Keep it turned on!"

"Check in once in a while…"

Two days later, his younger brother, the Tween, also threw his dirty clothes in the wash pile without emptying his pockets. And, unfortunately, I also didn't check the pockets -- again.

As I heard him turning the house upside down looking for his phone, I put on my coat and grabbed the car keys. "Where are you going?" he asked.

"To the store, we're low on rice…"

ROCKIN' IN THE FREE WORLD

Women of my generation were trained early on -- when a Beatle walks in the room, you scream; no other response is appropriate.

So when I took the kids to see Ringo Starr play Radio City Music Hall in New York, as soon as the funny one (who is now a grandfather) walked on stage, I issued forth a scream — much to the mortification of my sons. Not even their adulation for the Beatles was a sufficient antidote for the embarrassment of your mom screaming like a public ninny.

It wasn't until I looked around and saw some other middle-aged women waving their arms and screaming, "We love you, Ringo!" that I realized this perhaps was unsuitable behavior for adults over the age of 19. But these women are me. I am them. We are old. Kookookachoo.

It was cool to be a part of history, one that my kids appreciate, even though it is ancient history to them. This may be the last concert we ever attend together.

Our Teenage Daughter is the age where going to a concert with her mom is about as appealing as…well, as going to a concert with her dad.

It happened so quickly. I miss the good old days of escorting her to Miley Cyrus concerts, with special guests the Jonas Brothers! It seems like just last year she went with another family to see Taylor Swift. Actually, it was just last year.

Now she wants to go to hipster venues and see hipster bands I've never even heard of. Nothing makes you feel older than talking to your teenage daughter about music. (The kids today! With their hair and their music!)

Last week, she wanted to know if she could go see Vampire Weekend and Of Montreal. I stood there and blinked, momentarily stumped. I wanted to pick Of Montreal because it sounded less threatening than Vampire Weekend. (Montreal is a lovely French Canadian city with many quaint shops and bistros. Vampires suck your blood.) But Vampire Weekend was playing Radio City Music Hall and I know what that is. (It's where Ringo sings.) Of Montreal was at Terminal Five and I don't know what that is except I drove by once and saw all these Goth kids waiting to get in – are they still called "Goth kids"?

While negotiations were underway, Vampire Weekend sold out so that was that. If we were going to let her go, it was going to be Of Montreal. At Terminal Five. With the Goth. But I liked the kids she was planning to go with (not a Goth in the bunch) and one of the moms (also not a Goth) was picking up afterward.

I told my husband.

"Absolutely not. No, she can't go to Montreal," he said, "she's just a kid!"

"It's a band. They sing that Outback steakhouse commercial."

"It's a what? They sing the huh? In the where?"

"What's the matter with you? Pay attention."

Let's have bizarre celebrations, I sing.

*Let's go to Outback and have steaks tonight...*I improvise.

I remind him that this is not her first concert. "Over the summer, we let her go see Panic Room."

"They're called Passion Pit!" our Teenage Daughter yells down the hall in an exasperated tone.

"Right, Passion Pit," I call back. "They are beast!"

"Mom, don't say 'beast,'" begs our Teenage Son.

"Well, they are," I say.

"Yes," my husband agrees, "Pumpkin Patch are the beastiest."

Our daughter thinks I am, as the kids say, strictly L-7. (Did kids ever say that?) But I've been around --

I remember when I was nine, Sue Schmidt's parents took us to see David Cassidy at Madison Square Garden. I wore a party dress and patent leather party shoes and screamed so much I popped my chain belt.

Once, when I was 16, my mom, who was pretty strict, let me go with friends to see Jethro Tull even though I had to re-take the SATs the next day. That was pretty shocking. I guess she wanted me to relax and not stress about it. I went to see Tull (who I didn't even like) – they played a forty minute set with no encores, lots of booing, and got me home early.

My math score went up 100 points the next day. Maybe Of Montreal will help our daughter with French. *Bien sur!*

THAT NICE VAMPIRE NEXT DOOR

Teenage girls love three things: hiding in their rooms, texting each other constantly, and eternal, undead creatures of the night.

There was a teenage rush to the box office when the new vampire movie came out based on the Twilight Saga books. Of course, teenage girls and vampires have a lot in common. They're moody and it's impossible to get them out of bed in the morning. One big difference through – vampires avoid mirrors.

I had the thrill of picking up four teenagers who had watched *Twilight* at the multiplex Saturday night. They screamed much of the way home. I don't know why since they never finished a sentence.

"Didn't you think Edward [a sullen vampire boy in love with Bella, a sullen non-vampire girl] was so...eeeeeeeeeee."

"That part where he was all sparkly...AAAAH"

"What was that? He's so cute, aaaaaaaah! Eeeooooooh!"

"I wonder how they'll show what happens in the second book when they make the next movie?"

"Why, what happens?"

"EEEEEEEEE! You haven't read book two?"

"Aaaaaaaaaaaaaaaa!"

"Well, tell me, I want to know."

"You don't want to know. Oh my gosh, she hasn't read it. EEEEEEE!"

"AAAAA!"

"WAAAAA!"

"EEEEEE!"

At this point, I pulled over to pump some gas and regain my hearing. I haven't read the books. I asked my friend Julia who read the first book if it was appropriate for our girls. She said, "Yes, if you enjoy unbelievably derivative plot-lines, ham-fisted writing, and deadly boring, unoriginal fiction." She compared it to eating food that's already been eaten.

But she's not in high school.

No one said that the *Twilight* series was original. Why, we had Gothic plot-lines and romance aplenty in *Dark Shadows*, the late 1960s/early-'70s soap opera about the vampire Barnabas Collins who, if I remember correctly, found time to be quite the ladies' man about the estate. I was nine and watched because I thought Quentin the Werewolf was cute.

Later, I saw Frank Langella as *Dracula* on Broadway. I was a teenager and I swooned. If there had been the expression "mad hot" back then, I would have used it.

What is it with teenage girls and vampires?

It seems that girls are hoping for a little romance in the future and, consequently, the chivalry we thought was dead may be forced to reanimate like a thirsty vampire on a moonlit night.

Take Edward, the *Twilight* vampire, for example. Edward is a nice boy, a "vegetarian" vampire whose family has agreed to drink only animal blood and spare the humans they live amongst. That may not sound very vegetarian to an actual vegetarian but, for a vampire, it's a huge effort. And it means so much to his girlfriend Bella.

I caught my daughter and her friends checking out a website called "40 Edward Cullen Characteristics Every Guy Should Have." Some of the characteristics that make Edward so great are predictable from a teenager's point of view: He can drive 200 kilometers an hour and is "inhumanly attractive." But there were surprises on the list.

Apparently, the perfect guy should have these vampire qualities:

- be a gentleman
- be really smart
- smell extraordinarily nice
- have eyes only for you even if he is surrounded by hot girls
- quote Shakespeare
- stand in front of you in a protective way when you are in danger
- give you his jacket when you are cold
- have morals
- love you for what you are inside, not for how you look
- be charming
- sparkle in the sunlight
- have a nice family
- always pay for everything
- have been pretty much single since 1901
- hold your face while he kisses you.

I love it. Not a word about his pants sagging two feet below his underwear waist band or that he must grunt like a dolt instead of speaking in clear sentences. As our Teenage Daughter ventures into the dating world she could do a lot worse than going steady with a creature of the undead.

TEENAGERS DOWN ON THE FARM

Our Teenage Daughter urgently asked me to look over some information from her high school announcing an opportunity for students to spend a week on a farm. "Mom," she said, "It's always been a dream of mine to live on a farm." Really?

I knew about her love of Broadway shows, her fondness for Lady Gaga, and her weakness for *Arrested Development* reruns. But goat birthing? This was the first I'd heard of it. She never expressed any interest in farming before. Maybe it was the endless hours spent on Facebook that did it to her. All that Farmville.

It turned out the farm was about an hour away, the fee reasonable, and she would be required to do all her school work for the class days missed. How would she fit it all in? No cell phones, no texting, no TV, no headphones, no Internet except for brief emails to parents. Those electronic constraints guaranteed the liberation of several hours a day.

Before she left, we needed to outfit our suburban farm girl correctly. The packing list specified "farm pants, 2 pair."

What are farm pants? She wondered. Think flannel-lined, regular cut blue jeans. Not jeggings. Not pencil jeans, not stretch jeans. She tried them on and looked adorable, like Doris Day in the 1950s. "Look how high they come up, mom!" "Yes, dear, that's called your waist. Clothes used to come up to there. It's very practical for birthing goats."

She also brought hand warmers, flannel shirts, a fleece hat, warm jammies, and a sleeping bag. She needed a flashlight since the bathroom was in the next building. She brought one towel. "Hang it up," I told her, "or it won't last."

Over the week she helped birth many baby goats (apparently they need to be caught when they emerge), fed them, milked cows, shoveled manure, and carried 50 pound feed bags. And she palpated a cow. That meant she had to put her entire arm inside a cow. Sounds awful, right? Imagine how the cow feels about it. "Freaky, but cool," was the review. (From our Teenage Daughter, not the cow.)

We got a few other emails in the course of the snowy week.

"Love the farm. Getting up at 5:30 and wearing all my clothes at once to keep warm."

"See you soon. Gotta clean the barn before milking!"

"Another goat was born today and is nibbling on my face. So cute!"

Finally, she came home with a duffel bag full of clothes that smelled like a barn. "Don't they smell great?" she asked. "But they are covered in goat placenta." Does Tide get out goat placenta?

I threw the whole bag downstairs to the laundry room.

"I had the time of my life," she said, stashing away a year's supply of goat cheese in our fridge. We've never needed much more than a week's supply before...

"We had fresh baked bread every day with fresh preserves. It was so good. Why don't you bake bread, Mom? It's really easy."

I brought out the welcome home dinner I'd prepared – a big, juicy steak.

"Mom, are you crazy -- I can't eat this!"

"Why not?"

"From now on, I'm a vegetarian."

I guess once you've fed it, milked it, and palpated it…it's hard to eat it.

HAPPY BIRTHDAY, RODAN

Planning a birthday for a teenage girl has its challenges. So many questions—

Will boys be involved?

Probably.

Will my daughter think whatever I plan is lame?

Yes.

Does she even want me to plan her birthday?

No.

I remember my 15th birthday and how my parents tried to make things special for me. That was the year they rented a 16mm movie projector and let me order a movie for my friends to watch at our home.

[Note to readers under 40: This was a really big deal. A movie, shown in your house? Yes, there were no DVDs or videos, no Netflix, no Redbox, no downloading on your laptop, iPhone, iPod, or personal electronic device of any kind!]

Inexplicably, I chose the Roger Corman film, *The Raven*, with Vincent Price, Peter Lorre, Boris Karloff and, inexplicably, a very young Jack Nicholson.

A few hours before the party, which consisted of only girls since we Catholic high school students knew no boys, the equipment arrived with the film canisters. The company sent the wrong movie. No *Raven*. Instead, I got *Rodan*.

Rodan was a 1950s Japanese monster movie like *Godzilla*. I was disappointed but my dad was delighted. See, he'd been doing his Rodan impression for years. He often acted out his version of Rodan on the beach in the summers. He'd put on a deep, news announcer voice, put one hand to his ear as if he were broadcasting on the radio, and pronounce:

"Shortly after World War II, a group of Japanese scientists conducted a series of top secret experiments off a secluded island in the Pacific. The result? Roooodaaaan!"

Then he'd run down to the water's edge and pretend to be Rodan rising out of the sea. Eventually, he retired the Rodan impression. (Years later he was thrilled when I started producing grandchildren – it meant he could revive his old act. Rodan Lives!

I was not happy about the *Rodan/Raven* switch. I wanted my friends to watch *The Raven*. The company was called. Arrangements were made to rush over the proper film reels.

The doorbell finally rang and the delivery guy from the film company was cheered. *The Raven* was loaded onto the projector (another half hour process for anyone who has ever tried to thread a film projector). Everyone's nerves were shot, but we had fun.

"Hey!" I said to my Teenage Daughter. "Instead of some big party, how about you and I just get in our pajamas, eat ice cream, and watch old horror movies?"

Our Teenage Daughter rolled her eyes at me, and proceeded to take over the planning of her own party.

I guess she's too old now for her mother to throw her a birthday party.

No more Little Mermaid Princess parties with a dozen squealing girls running through the house.

Quoth the Raven, "Nevermore."

IS THIS ROUGHNESS REALLY NECESSARY?

O ur Teenage Son has started high school. He began this new chapter in his life with confidence, good cheer – and a very nervous mother. I'm just not ready for conflicts, the danger, the violence my son will surely be exposed to...

I'm just not ready for football.

He's ready – he's been ready for football since the day he was born. The first words my son heard on Earth were the doctor examining the 12 pound, one ounce bundle and proclaiming, "Hoo boy -- this one's a football player!" Actually the first thing he exclaimed was, "Dear God, this baby is 12 pounds!" The second thing he exclaimed was, "Hoo boy – this one's a football player!"

The kid loves the game. Not me. Seeing the boys out there on the gridiron clanging their helmets together (with their heads inside) makes me woozy.

You know that little jumpy feeling you get in the pit of your stomach when you see your toddler running ahead on the sidewalk and tripping and skinning his knee? Add ten years, now that toddler's a teenager. Now he's not just skinning his knee – he's deliberately and repeatedly slamming into other large kids, flying through the air, landing on his head (or some other kid's head). That maternal jumpy feeling is now a total, non-stop freak-out.

Oh, outwardly I'm calm, cool, and collected: "Good play, son! Way to crush the other guy's spleen!" But inside, I'm losing three years off my life expectancy with each game.

Not that I don't have some appreciation for the game. My dad loved football. But he hadn't played the game since his days in Brooklyn as the 14-year-old quarterback of the Gerritsen Beach Gaylords (which must have sounded a lot tougher in the 1940s).

He took us to West Point games, and taught my sister and me the finer points of the NFL most Sundays. We'd toss the ball around and, at Thanksgiving, we'd play touch football with the cousins. But these were casual, goofy games. No one was out to bash in someone's brains.

Our son started playing in seventh grade. At the first game I attended, a boy was carried off the field on a stretcher and whisked away in an ambulance. Luckily, he only had a bruised rib.

My son tried to calm me down: "Oh, don't worry about me. See, that kid was the biggest kid on our team so, of course, the opposition was going to try to take him out. I'm, like, the fifth biggest kid. There are at least four bigger guys before they even get to me."

I decided to gently suggest to my son that he take up some after-school activity that would be less heart attack-inducing for his mother.

"Hey, I know a really cool sport. How about Quidditch?" I casually mentioned over dinner one night.

"What's Quidditch?" his father asked. The whole family dropped their forks and stared at him in disbelief.

"Uh, Dad -- helloooo, Harry Potter?" said our Tween.

"Harry Potter what?"

"It's the sport they play at Hogwarts School," I explain, feeling superior having read the first four books.

My husband stared blankly.

"Quidditch is the sport where you fly around on broomsticks and chase a flying magical golden ball called a snitch."

My husband blinked a few times. Then, his brow furrowed.

I sighed. "Okay --Muggles, or non-wizards, run around with broomsticks and the person who plays the snitch runs away from them and tries not to be caught. The team positions are beater, chaser, and keeper and they all basically do what they sound like they should do. The snitch can and does leave the field and runs through the stands while the players can't. It's sort of like soccer, polo, lacrosse, and ice hockey -- but not really."

My husband's head remained oddly immobile, but his eyes started glazing over. "Uh huh," he said. "Why didn't you say so?"

I turned my attention back to our Teenage Son. "I think some colleges are actually recruiting for Quidditch teams now..."

He was unmoved by my brilliant idea. So now, we're onto junior varsity high school football (some players have beards!) Oh, I'll go to the games and I'll cheer. But maybe I should wear a helmet. Backwards. That way I can't actually see the game.

ANOTHER OPENING, ANOTHER SHOW

My husband is a comedian. I don't mean that as a pejorative; I mean he is a professional comedian. He's been in show business all his life. I was in show business, briefly, when I was 9 years old. Cathy Curtin and I had an act. We sang *Raindrops Keep Falling on My Head*, and we did a time step. We performed a couple of times at senior citizen homes, but we got no offers from Broadway so we broke up the act.

So it was only a matter of time before our kids caught the bug. My husband laid down the law: they can do all the summer theater camp and school plays they want but no going into show business professionally until after they get through college. He was a professional child actor. So he's got the inside dope. "Kids shouldn't be in show business. All children's roles should be played by robots or trained chimpanzees!"

So our kids are in theater camp.

Our Tween was in the middle school play, *Hippie Flower Power*, a global warming retelling of Woodstock. Yes, the script was as bad as it sounds (well, maybe a little worse than it sounds) but the kids were great and had fun. They had fun because they were on the stage and not in the audience. His Teenage Sister was a counselor for the ten-year-olds, helping to produce their musical, *Westward Whoa*, a rip snortin' melodrama of the Old West.

Westward Whoa was very cute I think it had something to do with horses. The children really gave it their all --singing, dancing, acting, ropin', ridin', and do-si-do-ing all over the place.

At night, the teenager counselors had their own musical. This year's production was *Rent*, the rock musical about bohemian artists in New York City who, apparently, do not want to pay their rent.

During his opening night curtain speech, the director told us, "There is some 'content' in *Rent*. And if we took out all the 'content,' it wouldn't be *Rent*."

I guess it would be *Westward Whoa*.

I never saw *Rent* when it ran on Broadway but all the theater camp parents had already heard about "content" issues with the play from their kids who were in the cast. They all came home telling us that there were some things in the show that might be "inappropriate." I think the kids were more uneasy than the parents.

After all, it's not as if we grownups haven't been around for forty or more years, as if we didn't live through the exact era in the play. Hard for some of our kids to believe, however. I told my daughter I might be able to help her come up with an authentic costume for the play's Alphabet City setting and late 1980s era since I was a fashion editor at a teen magazine during those years.

"Yeah, but really, Mom. Really? But you weren't exactly, you know, Avenue A."

So uncool mom went to the opening night, waved to the pastor of our church, and then slouched down in my seat as our children paraded content all over the stage: AIDS, addiction, sexual orientation, disdain for the suburbs, edgy opposition to "the man." I squirmed, I blushed, I winced, my scalp itched.

Could we do *Oklahoma!* next year? It's got a girl who can't say "no," a peddler selling chemicals you sniff to have wacky dreams, and several attempted murders.

On second thought, maybe they should just do *Westward, Whoa!*

CAN WE CHANGE THE CONSTITUTION SO I CAN BE PRESIDENT?

I can't find my birth certificate.

I'd been working toward my longstanding promise to our Teenage Daughter for a trip to Paris when she turned sixteen and figured I should start by finding my passport. (That's also the cheapest part of the whole deal.)

I hadn't seen my passport for a while – once I started having kids. I'm lucky if I get out of the house, much less out of the country. When I did finally find it (it was in the last place I looked), I thought, "You know, everyone complains about their passport photo, but I look pretty good!"

Of course I did – my passport expired 14 years ago! Yes, my love of travel, foreign and domestic, has clearly been seriously curtailed in the years since we had four children.

So I went to the post office and helped our daughter apply for a passport but, when the postal worked looked at my form, he asked. "Where is your birth certificate?"

I said I didn't have one, but here was my expired passport, driver's license, and marriage license.

He looked at my application. "Birthplace says France."

I started getting nervous – over-explaining the way you do when you're completely innocent but, for no reason, you think everyone thinks you're guilty.

"That's right," I said. "See, my dad was working there when I came along. But my parents were both Americans, from Brooklyn and Queens. Well, my dad was from Brooklyn, my mother from Queens, and I--"

"You need to show that you are a citizen."

"Well, here's my expired US passport."

He said that it was so old it was as if it didn't exist.

"But it exists, here look. My passport expired, but I didn't!"

He sighed, then urged me to return with the proper paperwork. Then he started stamping some papers with a rubber stamp. I was convinced those papers were just there to be stamped for emphasis, to let me know our conversation was over.

I reluctantly called my mom to ask if she had my original birth certificate. I was reluctant because I had a feeling she had given it to me at some point.

"I gave it to you when you got married. Don't you have a metal box?"

My mother is much more organized than I am. She always kept important papers in a metal box. I have a metal box too. I'm just not sure where it is. I mean, I know it's in the house somewhere.

I had to dig out the old cardboard boxes of files and papers in our basement that got packed when we moved but never got unpacked. Eleven years later.

As I searched, I came across a treasure trove of my past including loving notes from my mom when I first was away at college. They said, "Just be happy, and I'll be happy." That's the way I feel about my kids now.

There were exuberant letters I wrote from Europe when I was a student abroad at age 20. My tone reminded me of our daughter's now, always so excited and enthusiastic about new experiences. My parents kept the letters and returned them to me so I would have a record of my trip.

I also found rejection letters from Harvard, Princeton, and Yale, artwork from my kindergarten class, and a first aid award for knowing how to treat a snake bite. For those without a first aid award, it involves matches, a sharp knife, suction, and a healthy spitting reflex. But no birth certificate.

Ultimately, I had to sit down and write an email to the village hall outside Paris where I was born, in my rusty French, (*merci beaucoup*, Google Translator) asking if they could send me an official birth certificate, *s'il vous plait*.

The French civil servants wrote back to say they couldn't send my birth certificate without seeing my passport. I explained I didn't have a passport and couldn't get one without a birth certificate. We went back and forth until I finally convinced the Nation of France that a scan of my expired passport and information about my parents' dates and places of birth might seal the deal.

Eventually, an envelope arrived with my birth certificate. Three weeks after that, my new passport was delivered with my new passport photo. Bad photo. It looks like a female impersonator disguised as me for Halloween. I tried to get them to use my old, young passport photo -- "just Photoshop in a little gray," but they wouldn't go for it. Now, I can travel and I know how to treat a snake bite. Eat your hearts out, Harvard, Princeton and Yale!

PARIS FROM MOM TO DAUGHTER

S o, in spite of the economy, our busy schedules, and the fact that a teen and her mom can get on each other's nerves, we made the reservations, left my husband in charge of the three boys, packed our new passports, grabbed my sister (the "Fun Aunt"), and off we went.

Paris was...very Parisian. I lived there for six months as a student in the '80s, but it was the six months of the year where it is always dark and cold and rainy. On this trip, the sky was bright and endless, the architecture incredible, the river sparkled, the streets and the cafes bustled with activity. My daughter kept saying she felt like she was in a movie. So did I. (A French movie – but you already knew that.)

Our hotel was quaint and we made a challenge of trying to get the snooty French lady at the front desk to smile once a day. But what's a vacation to France without a snooty French lady? The elevator was so tiny, the three of us couldn't fit. We got used to running up three flights to our rooms where we'd throw open the French doors and listen to the street sounds until we fell asleep.

We walked everywhere or took a boat that shuttled up and down the river Seine, letting us off at key sites like the Eiffel Tower, the Champs Elysees, the Latin Quarter. We climbed to the top of Notre Dame Cathedral one clear morning and looked out at the city with a gargoyle eye view. Quasimodo had nice digs.

At the Louvre, we rushed through the galleries to find the Mona Lisa. "You've got to see it," I told my daughter. "It's the most famous painting in the world! Nat King Cole did a song about it!" After negotiating the crowds standing before the surprisingly small masterpiece which is under glass, she wandered away to the other side of the room and stood transfixed in front of a huge painting depicting the Emperor Napoleon crowning his queen, Josephine, witnessed by shocked and irked clergy and nobles. She spent a long time taking in the scene: "It's incredible. The detail. Everyone is doing something different."

As opposed to the Mona Lisa who, let's face it, just sits there. Smiling.

Later, I enjoyed watching her sit in a café thoughtfully writing out long post cards to her friends, instead of texting short missives every 90 seconds. The impracticality of her having a phone in Europe (we shared one emergency phone) made it actually possible to bond uninterrupted.

In one neighborhood, I tried to lead us down a street where I lived as a student. My Teenage Daughter was (surprisingly) not interested in standing outside an apartment building, looking up, and reminiscing about ancient history. She takes after her father. When I dragged my husband to my 20th college reunion, I spent a good deal of time walking around campus telling him, "Oh, that building wasn't here when I was here, but that one was." After a couple of hours of this, my husband finally announced, "Okay, okay! I get it. When you went here, the new buildings weren't here and the old ones were." Some people just don't enjoy architecture.

My Teenage Daughter wasn't in France to relive her mom's memories, she was there to make her own. Riding bicycles around the gardens of Versailles at dusk, past the descendants of Marie Antoinette's sheep; finding a lady singing Edith Piaf songs in a bistro hidden down an alleyway (I know –ridiculous, but it happened! I'm surprised that lady wasn't singing Piaf while eating a baguette and snails!); being mistaken for French by a salesgirl in a chic boutique and smiling and nodding until I came over to translate.

I looked over my shoulder at my old address and smiled at the memory of my college days. Then I turned and ran to catch up with my daughter who was already walking ahead. *C'est la vie!*

GLITTER GLUE REMBRANDT

G litter glue: the messy medium preferred by parent-hating arts and crafts teachers at day camps everywhere. If you have a toddler, you've got glitter glue. All over the place. Our house is beginning to look like Studio 54. [Note: For you younger readers, "Studio 54" was a disco where Liza Minnelli partied in the 70s. "Liza Minnelli" is an entertainer. She is the daughter of Judy Garland. "Entertainment" is what used to make up show business before reality television. "Judy Garland" played Dorothy in *The Wizard of Oz*. *The Wizard of Oz* was a movie. Not with Seth Rogan.]

On one particularly glitter glue-challenged morning, I found myself crying out for help – I called another mom friend of mine. "My little guy is so happy at his new summer camp but if he comes home with one more craft involving 'glitter glue,' I'm going to climb a tower with a rifle."

Since my Toddler started at preschool camp, nearly every afternoon has yielded a piece of construction paper with foam objects attached and heavily layered with gallons of glitter glue. There's been a lot of red, white, and blue in a patriotic nod to our nation's birthday.

My house is not very neat. And by "not very" I mean "not." I have four kids, a dog, and a cat -- not to mention a husband -- so a little glitter glue can actually enhance the appearance of my decor. But a lot of glitter glue...is a lot. We all love our children. But just how long (if at all) do we have to keep their art projects?

My friend Mimi has two young ones at the camp so she gets twice the glue projects coming home. She pledges to take them no further than the garage. Her husband can go look at them there. Their garage is a glitter glue art gallery, but now their house is mercifully glitter glue-free.

Another mom friend of mine admits she keeps a trash can in the garage and, after she scoots the kids into the house, the day's artwork goes from the car directly into the can. So far her kids have never asked, "Hey, where's that glitter glue portrait of Patrick Henry I made today?"

My neighbor tells me she displays the kids' artwork proudly on the mantle until, after a day or two, it simply disappears. Mysterious.

While helping me with a recent paperwork purge at our house, our Tween noticed that I had several baskets of artwork by his younger brother but none of his.

I looked at him. He looked at me. He squinted. I blinked. Beads of sweat formed on my brow.

"That's because your brother's in preschool and brings home stuff every day. You're in fifth grade and don't bring home that much anymore."

He looked at me dubiously. I took him by the hand to the basement and opened the drawer of an old bureau to show him that I had saved an equally ridiculous amount of his masterpieces including a giant, hand-drawn mother's day card, early poetry and song lyrics, and a sketch of SpongeBob SquarePants on a napkin. (Could be worth something some day – after all, Picasso used to doodle on napkins...)

He gave me a big smile.

I also discovered that if you leave a glitter project on the floor of your car on a very sunny day, it gives the inside of your car a disco ball effect with bright spots all over the interior and passengers. Why you would want this, I don't know – but it's all part of living in a glitter glue world.

HAPPY BUCKETS

The boys were fighting over a toy in the car while I was driving. They were making me nuts. I told them to cut it out. The Toddler piped up, "It's time to get out your bucket, Mommy."

I had no idea what he was talking about. "My bucket?"

"Get out your bucket and fill it with happiness."

This must be something he learned in kindergarten. I had to laugh since he was absolutely the worst offender in the car, but apparently the problem wasn't their screaming and hitting, the problem was that my happiness bucket was empty.

His suggestion reminded me of the demonic child Rhoda in *The Bad Seed* who tells her mother – with a sickening, sweet smile -- she'll trade "a basket of kisses for a basket of hugs." Then she kills some poor guy who's on to her evil ways. [If you have never seen this classic film, you should if only for the experience of watching everyone yell their lines at the top of their lungs. They were all in the show on Broadway and they think they are on stage instead of in a movie. There are some astonishingly bizarre curtain calls at the end, too.]

The Toddler explained that they were reading a book in school about carrying buckets of happiness around.

I guess it's true that if we don't carry our happy buckets with us then we'll be less able to fill them when we come across some happiness. We'll have to hold small amounts of happiness in our pockets and bare hands and risk dropping the happiness, or it will slip through our fingers and spill out on the street, and we'll be stepping in happiness all day and getting it all over our shoes.

We got home and he ran to find the book. In the illustrations, happiness seems to be in sort of a magical fairy dust form that would definitely be hard to carry around without some sort of receptacle. Really a large Ziploc bag would probably make the most sense because you could trap the happiness inside. Or a very big purse that can hold lots of things like an extra pair of shoes if your heels start hurting your feet.

I appreciated my son's attempt to insert some happiness into my day. It might have helped if his happy bucket had been out when he was fighting with his brother so I wouldn't have kicked mine over in exasperation.

Isn't this how the Great Chicago Fire started? Mrs. O'Leary's cow knocked over her happiness bucket which banged into a lantern which burned down the barn, and the next thing you know – deep-fried Chicago. So if you have a happiness bucket, keep it away from cows.

GET ME TO THE SCHOOL ON TIME

When I was too young to walk to school by myself, my mom escorted my sister and me the two blocks to our school and always made sure we were there before the bell rang. Mom was prompt.

Once I was old enough to walk the short distance on my own, I managed to be late every day. I figured it was because I am not a morning person. I used to think my mom was a morning person. But she was just getting up to get me up. Now I get it.

So now, I am up early every morning shoving our kids out the door to get to school.

Why me? Why doesn't my husband get the kids out the door in the mornings? "You are a morning person," he says, sipping his coffee and reading his paper. "I am not. It takes me a long time to wake up."

Just because I have to get up early every day doesn't mean I'm a morning person. I'm not a morning person. I'm a person who gets up in the morning to yell at other persons to get up in the morning and go to school!

There are actual morning people. My sister has always been an early riser. When we were teenagers, it exasperated her when I slept 'til noon. She resented having to wait around for hours every weekend before I was ready to function. It wasn't my fault, I was just tired from all that getting up for school during the week.

My neighbor Marie is a natural morning person. She awakes at the crack of dawn, catches the early train with coiffed hair, perfect makeup, and a great outfit. She is cheery, peppy, and tops in her profession. (I, on the other hand, can usually be found at the bus stop embarrassing my Toddler because I'm still sleep-walking in my pajamas.) How the heck does she do it?

It must be something she eats. I asked her what she has for breakfast. "Nothing," she said. "I can't eat until later. Maybe a little juice, and no coffee."

No coffee? If I don't eat, I faint. If I don't drink coffee, people wish I had fainted.

I thought I had the solution in college: never take early classes. But I couldn't get up early enough on registration days to sign up for the later courses. So I'd get stuck taking 8 AM classes – with all the other lazy, groggy people who failed to wake up early.

These days, I make deals with myself when the alarm goes off. "If I get up, I can go back to sleep the second the kids leave." Of course I never do, but I'm so tired from lack of sleep I can't think straight so I fall for the same trick every morning.

Our four kids are eleven years apart from oldest to youngest. I did the math. I will be getting up early for school buses until at least 2023. So if you call me after 2023, please wait until a reasonable hour.

READING WRITING BITING: HOW NOT TO ANNOY YOUR NEIGHBOR IN KINDERGARTEN

I t came early this year. At the end of the second full week of school. The call from a teacher that begins, "There's been an incident."

"Your child has been bitten," said Mrs. M., my son's kindergarten teacher. "By a classmate," she quickly added. At least it wasn't a wolverine.

Luckily, I don't panic easily. This is our fourth kid we're talking about. It's not the first time I've had a bit kid. I was just glad he wasn't the biter. She told me that the skin was not broken and that no one seemed too traumatized by the affair. It started when my son spotted some Star Wars character on a backpack and wanted to point out to his friend that he knew which character it was. Shockingly, the little boy didn't care and, after about the fifth time my son pointed and insisted that his Star Wars trivia expertise be acknowledged, the other child finally bit the insistent finger, bringing the pointing to an end.

The finger was examined and deemed to be unworthy of a nurse's office visit so it was washed and dried and sent back to the blocks corner with the rest of my son still attached to it. The boys were spoken to and the biter apologized to the bitten.

The biter's mom called me that afternoon and was embarrassed. I told her no harm, no foul. We had met on the first day of kindergarten and our boys seemed to hit it off. She said her son was really not a biter, that no one in her family was a biter, and that biting other people was not characteristic behavior for her son who, she assured me, was usually not the biting kind. I said my son could drive a lot of people to uncharacteristic behavior.

This next morning, on our way to the bus stop, the Toddler said, "I don't like school. I want to stay with you." Perhaps it was because I was still in my pajamas and that looked like a good way to spend the day.

"Is everything all right at school?" I asked. "Isn't it fun to play? Don't you like rest time?"

"I got a sticker for resting really quiet," he said.

"That's so good. Maybe you'll get another today."

He thinks about it.

"Are you still friends with that boy who bit you?" I ask.

"Yes, he's my buddy."

"OK, well then, don't annoy him."

"I won't."

"I put Cheerios in your lunchbox."

He smiles. When the bus arrives, he hops on happily.

I go home to shower and dress, much to the relief of my neighbors. I savor the sense that the problems of my five-year-old's world are small today – as small as a finger fixed with a kiss.

WAY TOO MANY CARTOONS

I've watched an excessive amount of kids TV shows in the past sixteen years. With four kids, I've logged 17 million hours of cartoons. As a parent, I go back to old school mid-nineties: *Shari Lewis & Lambchop, Teletubbies, The Hugabug Club.*

The Hugabug Club wasn't around for long but it left a lasting impression. It starred the Landers Sisters - a couple of aging "models," twin sisters who had been on the cover of *Playboy* (Really? Really? Yes, really…). They danced around with full-body puppets of a non-descript furry nature, and I think they were in outer space. From time to time, Jonathan Winters would appear and tell a story. I know this sounds like a drug flashback but I never did drugs – I'm guessing that the producers of *The Hugabug Club* did plenty.

Our Toddler is on his own though. It's not the years of bad animation or incomprehensible plots that have worn me down. It's the recycling! Every other cartoon produced for kids over the past 20 years has been about recycling. After watching, with his three older siblings, six million cartoons encouraging us all to recycle, I've pretty much had it. These days I rarely watch what the five-year-old is watching -- unless it's SpongeBob (he of the square pants).

SpongeBob catches your attention with great writing and animation that is easy on the eyes (as opposed to say, Japanese anime which is migraine-inducing). With most other non-SpongeBob cartoons, I can't even tell what is happening. Like *The Misadventures of Flapjack*. I think it's about a boy who lives in a whale and has adventures and eats candy. For no apparent reason the whale talks like Pearl Bailey. It's a sassy whale.

Ben 10 is a boy who turns into an alien and then hangs out at a hot dog stand. The show looks very post-apocalyptic and creepy. You half expect Charlton Heston to run through screaming (spoiler alert), "Soylent Green is people!"

Jimmy Neutron is always blowing stuff up and getting away with it because his parents are dumb and oblivious. It's educational -- if your kid wants to grow up to be an arsonist.

We had some pretty bad cartoons when we were kids. Like *Josie and the Pussycats in Outer Space.* Just what our space program needs: girl rock stars with "long tails and ears for hats." They just don't write lyrics like that anymore!

Then there was *Speed Racer* who I thought was cute even though he was a bit one dimensional (well, actually, two dimensional). He was always gritting his teeth and sweating and everything in every episode seemed to revolve around how fast he could drive.

"The world may end – I'd better drive faster. The diplomat's daughter has been kidnapped – I must drive faster. The price of milk is rising – faster!"

We also had *Davey and Goliath*, everyone's favorite claymation Bible lessons. They were like Gumby and Pokey with a message and Davey had to learn a moral from his talking dog every week.

And there was *Gigantor* which was a gigantic (hence the name) flying...thing. A robot? A dinosaur? Can't remember, but I could sing the song. Gi-GAN-tor, Gi-GA-AN-tor!

So I don't watch cartoons with my Toddler anymore – except for SpongeBob. SpongeBob is always happy, almost. He loves his job, is friends with everyone, always looks at the bright side, and teaches good lessons. Like its okay not to know how to tie your shoe -- you will learn. But the major draw is that this cartoon mentions nothing about recycling. Bikini Bottom, where SpongeBob lives, even has landfills under the sea.

Al Gore wouldn't like it, but SpongeBob seems happy.

KINDERGARTEN DELINQUENT

I have attended my fair-share of parent teacher conferences. They're usually painless. With our youngest in kindergarten, I expect to be in and out with his teacher in a matter of minutes.

After all, barring a few minor issues, they're good kids.

Well, there was the time our daughter went on a kiddie crime spree stealing Fiskars, those child safety scissors, from her classroom. I found them all over the place, even buried in our backyard. It wasn't until said child attempted to give herself a haircut that I caught on to her compulsive school supply embezzling.

We spoke to the head teacher, tears were shed (by me), and our daughter has been on the straight and narrow ever since.

Another of our kids was caught stealing, but it wasn't material objects. It was focus. He had a thing about being the class clown. Some might call it Attention Deficit Disorder. We call it a being a wise guy. One routine involved him putting crayons in his pants during phonics. This was a slight improvement over his classic "putting crayons up his nose during phonics" act.

Despite that family history, I frankly expected to breeze through our kindergartener's meeting. Unfortunately, the teacher had a list -- a long list.

"He growls."

"He pretends to be a monster and scares the other children."

"He lies on the floor."

"He licked someone's shoe."

"He is resistant to the Golden Rule."

Apparently, my child would be an excellent candidate for home schooling or the Army. I try not to glance at my watch. How much more could there be?

"He doesn't recognize alphabet letters."

"What!?" Now this I can't believe.

Only days earlier I had been impressed when he picked up an alphabet book and read it to me without hesitation, reciting the letter, identifying the corresponding picture, and pronouncing the sound.

A apple ah

B ball bah

C cat cah

D dog dah

The whole alphabet.

I wondered if she had him confused with another child. Maybe he was just holding out on her.

I asked her if she was doing the letters in order.

No, she was asking about them randomly.

"Well there you go. He is waiting for you to go in order." I figured it was a problem on her end.

"Do you work with him, read to him?"

I blinked. I stared. Beads of sweat formed on my brow.

He's our fourth – we're somewhere between spoiling him and ignoring him. We're tired! We're old! His older brothers and sister can read to him, right?

Oh my God. We're the worst tired old parents in the world…

We vow to read with him on a regular basis. We pick a book.

Jesse Bear, what will you wear? What will you wear in the morning?

Apparently, Jesse Bear is indecisive about clothing when he wakes up.

"Wait," says our Toddler, "who is the author and illustrator?"

Smart as a whip, this kid is. Within a few days, he is much improved on his letters and has memorized the Golden Rule.

I send him back to school with renewed confidence.

"Give your teacher a break," I say. "And don't lick anyone's shoes!"

THINGS THAT MAKE ME GO GRAY

When our Tween said he wanted to do his homework with a friend who lived a few doors down, I did the quick inventory in my head. Lives on our side of the street, won't have to cross the road, all sidewalk to get there. That'll work. It didn't occur to me to say, "OK, but don't ride your scooter without a helmet while carrying your backpack on your shoulder and a notebook and pencil in your hand."

You can't vocalize every doomsday scenario that pops into your head. Can you?

So while my head was turned, off he went on his scooter, no helmet, school supplies hanging and dangling and generally getting in the way.

A little while later, there he was in the front yard, limping along, crying, bleeding. He pushed his scooter with one hand, covering his face with the other.

Those first few seconds of having no idea what happened were far harder than what actually occurred. Once the explanation started, the panic (mine) began to subside -- even though teeth were involved.

I dispatched a sibling for an ice pack and soothed the victim while he told me how he'd flipped over the handlebars and landed on his front tooth – his permanent, big front tooth. Well, "permanent" until now.

What followed is the traditional post-crisis dance familiar to moms everywhere: scrapes were bandaged, words exchanged, tears shed, reprimands reprimanded and, the crisis dance finale – big hugs.

The doorbell rang. It was a couple of his little buddies who had witnessed the accident and had come to return his notebook. They had also found a piece of his tooth on the sidewalk. One boy showed us a tiny gray pebble. "Thanks, but I don't think that's it," I said.

They scampered off, intent on spending the rest of the day searching for the missing tooth (well, at least the rest of the next 10 minutes).

The cut on his forehead stopped bleeding and the ice helped the bump stay down. We had a talk about helmets and multitasking while driving.

When our dentist took a look at the tooth, he was thankfully able, in less than an hour, to rebuild it. "That'll hold until the next time he knocks it out," he said. He'd raised two sons himself. (All of his teeth looked great. I caught myself wondering, "Who's his dentist?")

Being a mom is like being a crisis management director at some big company. Some big company where there are a lot of crises and I also happened to give birth to all the employees.

ROCKIN' IN THE FREE WORLD

Our kids have taken a lot of music lessons over the years. Piano, sax, trumpet, clarinet, recorder, ukulele, voice. Nothing has stuck. Oh, we sing in the car and dance in the kitchen and try to figure out how to play Christmas carols or pop songs on the keyboard. But no real musical genius in our family has emerged. I blame myself.

Musical talent always eluded me. And by "elude," I mean it ran away from me, hopped a cab, and fled to the other side of town. Then it checked into a hotel under an assumed name and hid under the covers.

We had a small orchestra at my school when I was about six or seven. Many children played the violin and caught on quickly. I took lessons for a time and loved carrying the violin case to and from school. The beautiful wood instrument nestled perfectly on the velvety inside, and there was a special place for the bow and rosin.

But actually playing it didn't go so well. I didn't understand the concept of drawing the bow across the strings to achieve a palatable sound. This, apparently, is the whole point of the violin – go figure. My mom was kind and used to compliment me on my practicing.

When I grew up – before I had kids of my own – I thought back on this and couldn't for the life of me figure out how my mom could have been so patient and encouraging. I mean, the sound I made with that violin made dogs wince, even elderly dogs that were hard of hearing.

Now that our Tween is trying out clarinet in the school band, I understand. He's inherited his mother's musical ability. I smile and encourage just like my mom.

Looking back, the horrible things I did to that violin weren't my teacher's fault.

Dr. Ma must have been a good teacher because he had a son named Yo-Yo who grew up to play the cello quite well. Maybe I should have tried the cello.

At one of our rehearsals, Dr. Ma handed me two mallets (no, he wasn't encouraging me to destroy my violin though I'm sure the thought crossed his mind). He sent me to play the xylophone. I'd always wanted a crack at that instrument. Dr. Ma asked me to play an "A." I looked at the keys and randomly plinked one note. He furrowed his brow. "No, no," he said. "An 'A.'"

I looked again and, hoping for the best, hit a different random key. (I mean, the odds were it could have been an "A.") Dr. Ma looked heavenward, held out his hand, and asked for his sticks back. That was the end of my xylophone career. Lionel Hampton would get no competition from me.

But lack of musical talent doesn't stop my kids. Especially if there is the possibility of turning a profit. One day, our Toddler took a cardboard box out onto the front lawn and placed it upside down. He went to the shed and got a low, folding beach chair and set it up at his makeshift "table". Then he went back in the house and got the bongo drums.

Then he asked me, "Mom, how do you draw one dollar?"

I showed him how to make the dollar sign and add the number one. He recreated it on a big piece of paper and grabbing the tape from the kitchen drawer, he went outside and stuck the sign on the front of the box facing the street.

Then he sat down in his beach chair and waited.

I wandered casually onto our front porch. "Whatcha up to, honey?"

"I'm waiting."

"What for?"

"Customers."

"What are you selling?"

"Bongo concerts."

I wasn't sure about the public at large but this I had to see. I found a dollar in my pocket and walked out to the sidewalk. I pretended to be strolling past, stopped, and took a long look at the sign.

"Excuse me, sir, I have a dollar here. What do I get for it?"

Trying not to smile, he said, "I will play for you."

"Okay," I said, handing him the money.

He stashed the bill under his box and then sat down in front of the bongos. Very seriously, he began to play. Now he definitely had the bongo method down, alternating hands, mixing up the tempos, cocking his head to one side in consideration of his composition.

After about 45 seconds, he stopped. I clapped. "That was very good."

"I want people to stop and give me dollars."

"A dollar's a little expensive. I don't know if people will pay that much."

"But the sign says a dollar."

"Very well." I went back in the house.

No one came. Finally, a woman jogged by and looked at the sign smiling but kept going. Our musician came into the house crying. "What's going on?" asked my husband, who had missed the whole start-up phase of the bongo business.

We explained the ups and downs of a new venture. My husband nodded sagely. "Let's take a look at that sign," he said, taking our son by the hand.

They took the sign down and markers were requested. "You're asking too much," my husband said. "Try five cents."

"Five cents?!" My musical genius was appalled.

"People will definitely pay five cents, and you'll get more customers."

Reluctantly, the dollar was crossed out and replaced with "5¢."

My husband strolled across the street where our neighbor's high schooler Danny was working in the yard.

Suddenly, Danny was on our sidewalk looking at the sign. "Here's a nickel," he said to our youngest. "Let's see what you've got."

Excitedly, our little entrepreneur began to bongo. Danny considered the brief concert. "Pretty good," he said, walking back across the street.

Amazingly, a few more neighbors with exact change came by shortly after my husband dropped in on them. Our son was in heaven and gave a dollar's worth of concert for each nickel.

"He was just overcharging," said my husband, who suddenly knew all about the music business.

As we watched the sun start to go down, we got ready to tell Mr. Bongos to close up shop for the night. A man came hurriedly down the block on his way somewhere. "Bongos! Five cents for bongo playing!" our son yelled, in a final sales pitch. "No time," said the man. "Sorry. Here." He tossed something on the box and kept going. Our son started jumping up and down. He turned around to where we sat on the porch. Waving his hand in the air, he showed us his final profit of the day -- a whole dollar.

LITTLE CAT FOUND

One Sunday morning, we were coming home from the store, the minivan loaded with kids, doughnuts, salty snacks, cookies, and other nutritional foods, when a frail feline attempted suicide by wandering aimlessly in front of our car. Then it sat down. Right in the middle of the road. Looking at us.

"C'mon," I said, slamming on the brakes. "Move!"

I got out and tried to shoo it out of the way. It just sat there. I thought if I tried to pick it up, it would run off, but it limply allowed me. It had rained the whole night before and the cat was a wet, dirty mess. But not in a tough, outdoor cat way. More like an indoor cat that had just spent the night outside with no idea what to do next. And no collar.

I put it at the side of the road and got back in the car. It just sat there.

"Mom, what are you thinking?" asked my Teenage Son.

"It's so pathetic and sad. If it's still there when I come back, I'm picking it up," I told him.

"And doing what with it?"

He had a point. We already had a cat and a dog, two fish and a turtle. We were over our quota of suburban pets. I couldn't help myself. I drove back by the playground ten minutes later hoping to see no sign of the little tortoise shell-colored cat. But there it was skulking under a couple of parked cars. I went over to it, hoping it would scamper off with some sign that it knew how to take care of itself.

Once more, it went limp and let me lift it up. Some moms in the park looked over. "Anybody know this cat?" I asked. Nobody did.

I put it down on my sweatshirt on the front seat. It just curled up and gazed at me. I drove over to the vet's office but no vets were on duty on a Sunday. I got another vet on the phone, but they were full up with strays and advised me to take the frazzled feline to the county pound.

I didn't want to take the kitty away from our village since I had a feeling it had a home there but was lost. I went back to my house and grabbed the cat carrier from the basement. I put in an old towel and transferred the cat from the car.

It was a sunny day so I set it on the porch with some food and water. The cat didn't eat or drink much. I kept thinking if it dried off and rested it would start purring, but it only moaned a sad meow.

Now the kids were on board with the kitty's plight, so they made signs that said "Cat Found" and we put them up on telephone poles.

We walked around knocking on doors because I knew by night we had to make a decision. Some people told us to bring the cat back to the playground because cats know how to find their way home. Having had my share of cats, I knew that was true -- but there was something about this one that seemed so helpless, confused.

It was getting late. No one knew of a neighborhood tortoise shell cat which made me think it was definitely a house cat. Or worse, someone had dumped it at the playground, and it had nowhere to go.

We were running out of options as we walked up a road over the hill from the playground. Again, no one recognized our description of the little cat. We were heading home when we passed a little dead end street, hidden away. As I knocked at the nearest house, I told the kids, "no matter what, this is our last door."

"Then what, Mom?" I hate when I don't have the answer so I was relieved when the lady of the house opened the door to distract us.

"Did you lose a little tortoise shell cat?"

"No, but the family in the last house up the street has been looking for theirs all day."

The kids were so excited, they ran up the hill ahead of me, as I thanked the occupant of the lucky last door. I puffed along after the kids just as a woman answered the door at the house, startled by my excited brood. "We found your cat!" They were jumping up and down.

"You did? Where?" Now she and I were also jumping up and down.

"At the park. We live up the road!"

"She's sick. She needs insulin. We've been so worried."

"We'll go get her."

We ran back to the car and drove home. I grabbed the cat carrier from off the porch. The kitty meowed mournfully.

"You're going home!" the kids told her.

We set the carrier on the front porch where the woman and her young children stood in the doorway. I opened the latch and the cat walked slowly into the house as if to say, "What a day."

"She never would have found her way home from the park," the woman said. "Can I buy you a new towel?"

"Oh, no," my Tween helpfully offered. "All our towels are old!"

I smiled and patted him on the head.

We got a card in the mail a few days later. It was from the cat. "Thank you so much for finding me and returning me to my family. My human brother and sister would be so upset if I didn't come home. Fondly, Wendy."

If I'd known she was able to write, I wouldn't have returned her.

FOR BETTER FOR WORSE NO
MATTER HOW ANNOYING

W hen I married a comedian, I got used to life being a little unpredictable and occasionally unorthodox. During our 19 years of wedded bliss,
my husband has worn a duck suit, walked through a carwash,
and ironed his pants in an elevator – all on TV.

He's traveled, but has intentionally never been a road com-
ic. As a dad, he wanted to be near us and has been able to ar-
range his career so it works for the family.

But suddenly, he found himself being booked to headline
on cruise ships so for a whole season he was gone just about
every other week. The job took him on some pretty exotic
trips. It was work, but I was jealous.

The funny part is that I love being away and traveling,
but he hates it. I love staying in different hotels and cities; he
needs his own bed and his special pillow.

But off he went to exotic locales where the time went much
more slowly for him waiting to perform at night, lounging
around during the day while, with my schedule at home, the

days flew by. Our kids are in four different schools -- we've got teen activities and kindergarten routines and middle school stuff rounding it all out.

Luckily, it's a lot easier to stay in touch than in the old days when you had to send a cable ship-to-shore. But there are still some quirks in the system. Phone calls from sea are expensive and Internet connections are unreliable, so we texted each other a lot.

Him: How are things at home?

Me: Parent/teacher tonight, root canal tomorrow.

Him: I'm sailing along Puerto Vallarta. The sunsets are amazing.

(Now he's noticing sunsets?) He never notices sunsets. At home, if I say, "Honey, come out here and look at this beautiful sunset," I usually get a grunt and the observation that "they've got one of those every 24 hours."

Me: Helping kids with homework. Hurricane science project should be the success of the sixth grade. A little math angst.

Him: Here, ocean, reading, food, napping, more food.

Me: Homework, dinner, baths, bedtime, alarm clock, bus, lunches, laundry. Went for the second part of my root canal just to relax!

Still, there were some positive things about having a spouse working out of town:

Complete control of the remote

The whole bed to myself (except for the dog and the cat)

Cereal for dinner (no cooking!)

Complete control of the remote

...but nothing beats having the whole family under the same roof.

Once my beloved returned from the sea, however, he immediately started to get on my nerves.

"Why isn't there any 15 grain bread?"

"The remote isn't where it's supposed to be."

"Where's my special pillow?"

I wonder if that's what happened with those whalers' wives back in the day, pining for their seafaring husbands, until they sailed back into town. Smelling like fish, insisting their poor wives make them a whale meat sandwich, then go out and swab the deck and hoist the petard...

Absence makes the heart grow fonder, until it comes home.

IT'S ALL DOWNHILL FROM HERE

On a family ski trip, the Toddler is lying face down in the snow. He is in Mini Moguls ski school which consists mostly of drinking hot chocolate and trying to learn the "pizza slice," the snow plow position that makes beginning skiers stop.

He doesn't want to do a pizza slice. He doesn't want to stand or move. He just wants to lie pitifully in the snow while bemused parents of more cooperative children ski around him.

Now this may sound like skiing is no fun. But I love skiing, my kids love skiing. Some days are just better than others. But once they get it, they love it. Within a week, that unruly child would be bombing the mountain from the top.

But you've got to catch the ski fever early. I did, skiing with my parents as a child. My husband never skied when he was young (apparently, not a lot of skiing in the Bronx). I tried to get him to like it as a slightly middle-aged dad. It didn't go well. He doesn't get skiing. Skiing doesn't get him. He hates skiing. Skiing hates him.

The ice, the low visibility, the frozen fingers and toes. My husband never understood the appeal. "What's the appeal?" he says. "You put boards on your feet, climb a mountain, fall down a mountain, then climb back up. What sadist invented this?" But my kids get it.

Watching our kids ski down a mountain, I can see them gaining strength and confidence. They encounter newfound freedom. Even the youngest go off with instructors and no micromanaging from mom and dad.

Parents stand below, squinting up at the snowy slopes, trying to pick out their children, waiting for them to come back to the base lodge. Then, at night, everyone is exhausted, appreciating good warm food, dry socks, and stories of the day's accomplishments.

The Toddler, on his second day, actually got up out of the snow at the request of his instructor. He sat on a bale of hay while the other tykes rode up the magic carpet, a small conveyor belt that took the kids to the top of an incline so they could ski down. On the last day of ski school, his instructor got him to do a pizza slice, nice and controlled as he descended the slope and came to a stop.

We all cheered! The kid's a natural.

Skiing as a family is not without effort. Everyone has to be zipped into overalls, snapped into boots, with mittens tucked into sleeves so no snow can touch skin. Helmets are then applied to protect against unruly teens on snowboards and other snow bunnies. (A "snow bunny" is someone who looks good in ski pants but has no idea how to ski down a mountain.)

You need a lift ticket to get up the mountain. You need a trail map to get down the mountain. Meanwhile, few activities can be more irritating than cramming a sticky toddler into snow pants. Chap Stik and Kleenex are not mandatory but are almost always needed. Then most children will inform you that they have to go to the bathroom. Everything is unsnapped and unzipped until the whole process can be repeated again.

But I remember being a city kid getting off the lift at the top of the mountain, hearing the wind, and seeing into the next state. I know my kids feel the same way as they push off and start the invigorating, liberating experience of finding their way home.

DOG GOES ROGUE, SCHOOL BUS WINS

Returning from errands one day, I turned into our driveway. My husband was doing yard work and our dog Cookie was sitting in the middle of our front lawn. She was beyond the spot where her long leash normally reaches, allowing her to sit on the porch and explore a bit of her domain. When my husband works outside, he lets her off the leash since he can keep an eye on her.

Unfortunately, a squirrel was bopping around on the other side of the street and, if there's one thing Cookie hates, it's squirrels. She dashed across the street to let that squirrel know who's boss and chased it to the safety of a curbside tree. Cookie then attempted to climb the tree. Unsuccessfully. It's probably the main reason Cookie hates squirrels – they can climb trees, and she can't.

I looked at my husband and gave him the "why is the dog not tied up?" look.

He looked at me with the "sorry, I will get her" look. He walked to the curb and called her.

"There's a school bus coming," I yelled. He tried to signal the driver that he was wrangling a dog. The driver looked at him uncomprehendingly. He called the dog. Cookie looked at him and waited. Just as the bus was chugging closer, Cookie must have thought, oh, okay he wants me to come back in spite of this large, yellow object heading this way.

So, she made a dash for it just as the bus was upon her.

"No!" yelled my husband.

The driver hit her brakes.

I screamed as Cookie ran right into the side of the bus.

There was a frozen moment when the bus just sat there, the windows filled with startled children. Then our dog limped out from behind the bus.

She hadn't yelped -- or I hadn't heard her with the yelling, the screaming, and the screeching -- so I wondered if she was even hurt. But I saw her holding up her back paw. I opened the side door of the minivan and she jumped in.

My husband consoled the driver. He told her to go ahead with the kids, the dog was okay, it was our fault, we were sorry.

Luckily, the animal hospital is right down the road and the vet saw me immediately. There was blood on the floor of the examining room and I noticed a cut on the side of Cookie's leg. A pretty deep gash but otherwise she seemed all right -- except she smelled terrible.

The vet explained that, in her fright, all available gas had come out of her body at the same time. It smelled like she had rolled in deer droppings for about a week. The gash we guessed was from hitting the wheel, maybe on a lug nut. Thank goodness the bus had been at a stop when she ran into it.

While she was examined, I called the bus company. The transportation director, who's been a friend since I moved to the rustic suburbs eleven years ago, came on the line, "How's your dog? I just heard." Her driver had radioed in the news. I love living in a small town.

"I hope the bus driver is okay," I said. She said school bus drivers are trained for dogs and deer and people and children and cars to leap into their paths. It showed.

Cookie got some stitches and a cheery neon-colored bandage that she promptly ate and then choked on. She also chewed out her stitches. She was moments away from the "cone of shame" head guard when the vet came up with miraculous (and terrible tasting) bitter apple drops that kept her from gnawing at her sore leg so it could heal. The minute we put them on, she left her wound alone with a sigh.

The next day, I met the afternoon bus with Cookie safely on a leash so all the children could see she was all right. The driver flashed her lights and put out her stop sign when she saw us standing there at the scene of the incident and pulled over.

"How's Cookie?" she asked.

"She's fine! Look!" We gave the driver flowers for saving our dog and she drove off. All the students peered out the windows. As the bus engine revved, Cookie backed up a little.

Cookie will spend the rest of the fall tied up on the porch looking longingly at those hated squirrels. The squirrels will no doubt taunt her. In the never-ending war between dogs and squirrels, the squirrels have won this battle. But Cookie will live to fight another day.

COMPETITIVE CHRISTMAS DECORATING: A SUBURBAN OLYMPIC SPORT

G rowing up in a New York City apartment, preparing for Christmas was pretty simple. We hung a wreath on the front door and we trimmed a small tree on Christmas Eve.

But when you move to the suburbs, you find out that decorating the house is a take-no-prisoners extreme sport.

First, there's the lead time. In our town, most families start decorating Thanksgiving weekend. I guess the rationale is that they'll take the long weekend to decorate the house and spend the remaining weeks until Christmas enjoying the fruits of their labor.

And one should enjoy them for many weeks because it is a complicated process that takes a lot of work. Our neighbors are up on ladders the Friday after Thanksgiving barely shaking off the turkey tryptophan, toiling away with power tools, lights, over-sized plastic lawn Santas, elves on the roof.....

After almost a dozen years of homeownership, when December rolls around, we usually still have a toothless, shrinking jack-o'-lantern from Halloween decomposing on our front step next to a pot of dead mums while everyone else has set up their grazing, motion-activated reindeer.

I am now in charge of putting up our outside lights. My husband finally abandoned the responsibility after years of waging losing battles with electricity. I don't mind. I find untangling wiring to be therapeutic.

Indoors, our Teenage Daughter ties ribbons to Christmas balls and we dangle those in the front window with some white lights. We Scotch Tape our Christmas cards around the archway that separates our living and dining rooms, and the boys unpack the special music boxes, baskets, and toy sleds that will cheer up (or clutter up, depending on your point of view) the living room until January. (Or should cheer up the living room until January but usually stay out until we are preparing for the Easter Bunny's arrival in April and we notice that there are still dusty toy sleds leaning up against the hearth.)

The pumpkin is dispatched to the dead pumpkin burial grounds (in lieu of flowers, the family asks that you get the dead mums off the front porch, too). The boys delight in throwing rotting pumpkins into the wooded ravine behind our house for small animals to eat. It's another lovely holiday tradition in the Konig household: the flinging of the moldy gourds.

Once the lights are up, we have to adjust our habits until the holidays are over. We cannot microwave in our house while the Christmas lights are on. It blows out the fuses. So we can either fit in with the neighborhood or we can enjoy hot food. But we cannot do both simultaneously. If I am in the kitchen preparing dinner and I need to nuke the vegetables, I yell, "Turn off the Christmas lights, I'm turning on the microwave!"

The main plug is pulled and then food is heated. "Restore power!" I command. The lights are plugged in again and to an outside observer, our décor must seem pretty unstable.

We gather around the tree, this year a fat one that is crammed into our small living room. It's obese. I would not have picked such a fat tree but we let the Toddler pick it out and that's the one he wanted. The kids also decided that they needed to put every piece of junk, er, artwork, they found in our Christmas decoration box on the tree. Every bent, old construction paper creation from the past sixteen years is on there. It's a mess. A fat, cluttered, happy mess.

I move some of the more heinous decorations around to the back of the tree when no one's looking. We sit by the fire and pop popcorn in the microwave. A circuit blows. The lights go out. It's beginning to feel a lot like Christmas.

GRANDPA AND SINBAD THE SAILOR

My dad loved telling adventure stories to his grand-kids. It is one of our favorite memories and brought us needed smiles after he passed away.

He'd pull a tidbit from a classic book he loved, like *The Adventures of Huckleberry Finn* or *Hans Brinker and the Silver Skates* or the tales of Sinbad the Sailor, and he'd sit them down and act it out. But it was entirely possible that he hadn't read these stories since he loved them as a boy, so the details he told my kids were his own.

One popular tale involved Sinbad getting shipwrecked in a strange land where he comes across an old man wearing a cloth, which my dad described as a diaper. This always got the kids giggling – a grown man in a diaper!

"Sinbad asks the old man to lead him to water and civiliza-tion, and the feeble man agrees, but only if Sinbad carries him on his shoulders. Even though Sinbad is weak from hunger and thirst, he lifts the old man onto his shoulders and heads off.

After a while, Sinbad suggests they stop to rest, but the old man tightens his surprisingly powerful thighs around Sinbad's neck, nearly choking him. Sinbad moves on and when they come to fresh water, the old man will not let Sinbad drink." "Keep moving, sailor! No stopping!" my dad squeals in a high pitched voice of the man in the diaper.

The children are rapt.

"Sinbad thinks he will die if he doesn't get away from this mysteriously powerful old man in a diaper. Then he spots a rare fruit hanging from the trees. Sinbad knows the potent nectar of that fruit will make the old man sleepy if he drinks it. Sinbad employs a little reverse psychology: 'Oh, I wish I had some of that delicious juice of the nub nub tree.'" (Here my dad would forget some of the details and start making up names and other plot points.)

"Oh yeah?" says the old man in the diaper. "Well, you can't have any. I can reach up and get all I want, and you just keep walking or I will choke you again." My dad would cackle fiendishly for added dramatic effect.

So the old man grabs fruit after fruit and greedily devours the nectar. "Sinbad waits for the man to get groggy and finally fall off his shoulders." The ending of the story would vary with each telling, but either way, Sinbad escapes and finds the nearby city in this strange land, where he amazes all with his tale of the old man in the diaper.

"Why, no one ever escapes the Old Man of the Sea," the citizens tell Sinbad. "He's killed hundreds of sailors. You are a hero." Then they introduce him to the king, who gives Sinbad half his land and his prettiest daughter.

By this point, our children were usually sitting there with their mouths hanging open at this marvelous turn of events. My dad would sit back, take a sip of his coffee, and look very satisfied.

The kids never got tired of hearing that story. My dad never tired of telling it.

OPERATION GOLF BALL FREEDOM

"**F**ree lemonade! Free lemonade!"
As we sat on my friend Julia's deck overlooking a shady river, we spotted a paper sign at the end of a small dock. A group of children had set up a lemonade business. Slowly, a regatta of canoes and kayaks approached, with friendly greetings to the children. Thirsty boaters floated for a while near the sugary sanctuary, chatting from vessel to vessel, and then paddled away with thanks and waves.

"Why didn't we think of that?" Julia asked.

"Who wants to see a couple of middle aged moms jumping up and down on a dock?"

"I mean for the kids..."

Actually, we set up quite a few lemonade stands when our older kids were younger. We'd spend a day just planning, painting signs, and building a makeshift stand. Chairs would be brought out and a tablecloth, followed by lots of ice and powdered lemonade. Whoever was the youngest was coerced into wearing a poster paper sandwich board and announcing the refreshing treat to neighbors and passersby.

The moms sat on the front lawn with our feet in a kiddie pool, filled to cool the children or curb boredom if sales were slow.

Julia and I did something every summer that was memorable. There was some viral Internet video about exploding bottles of Diet Coke by dropping Mentos mints into them. This always puzzled me since Diet Coke and Mentos were my favorite snack and I never exploded. At least not yet.

One day we went out on the lawn with a two liter bottle of Diet Coke and a roll of Mentos. The children couldn't believe we were about to do this. They cowered at a safe distance as we unscrewed the cap and readied the mints. "Watch out!" we yelled and dropped them in running away. A geyser of Diet Coke went up about ten feet in the air. We were soaked with soda.

"Do it again!" the kids demanded, laughing hysterically.

Last summer, we gathered at my dad's beach house. My dad hoarded golf balls. They were all around the house in baskets and buckets and bowls. Hundreds of golf balls. He didn't play golf but, for thirty years, he lived near a golf course and walked the back roads regularly. Every time he found a golf ball, he put it in his pocket. Whenever we visited, he would take his grandkids out adventuring and they would come back delighted after finding more golf balls to add to PopPop's collection.

Every summer Julia and her kids would join us at my dad's beach house for a few days. We'd joke that we should return the golf balls to the wild, setting them free. This was the summer we would do it. We emptied the balls into cloth bags and loaded up the trunk of the car. We drove out at dark to the edge of the golf course where the fence met the road. We got out and quickly put the bags down in the tall grass.

"Car!" one of the kids yelled. A car was coming and two women and six kids were standing by a golf course at night. It all had to look suspicious.

"Look!" I yelled, pointing up. "Look at all those stars!" Everyone looked up and started pointing, too. To the driver passing by, it looked as though we had pulled over to stargaze with the children. Or, rather, it looked like we were all over-acting, nervously pretending to stargaze.

Once the car disappeared down the road, we handed a bag to each kid, spaced ourselves out a few yards away from each other and waited for the signal. "One, two, three," the moms loudly whispered, everyone lifted their bags and dumped golf balls over the fence into the rough, returning them from whence they had come. The circle of golf ball life was complete. Some of those balls had been in my dad's house since I was a teenager.

We all rolled up our bags and dived back into the minivan. We drove off gleefully and fell out laughing in the safety of my dad's driveway.

The next morning, we returned to the scene of the crime. The balls were gone already – no doubt scooped up by a per-plexed groundskeeper. It didn't matter. We had set the golf balls free, back into their natural habitat. Operation Golf Ball Freedom – mission accomplished!

LIFE ON THE ARK

When our kids were little, we adopted a kitten. We figured cats were easy. Snowball grew up to be a wanderer who wanted to be outside all night. My husband and I found this extremely stressful since we grew up in the city and didn't know about outdoor cats. We waited up for her like she was a teenager and were greatly relieved when she rolled in at the crack of dawn.

Unfortunately, her reckless nightlife ended suddenly; she was playing in a pile of leaves out one night when an unsuspecting SUV parked on the poor thing. We immediately went out and got another kitten for the kids. This one luckily turned out to be a house cat who liked to sleep indoors. Much less stressful.

Once the three older kids were in school, we decided to get a dog. No family is really complete without a dog. First, my husband had to talk me out of a toy poodle ("That's not a real dog! A beagle is a real dog!"). I surfed the Web for local shelters and adoptable pups. I found a cute black mutt listed at a nearby rescue organization. It turned out to be a private home in a sketchy neighborhood where a family had dozens of dogs in their yard. It was a kind of rogue ASPCA -- well-meaning but not particularly organized. Our daughter caught the fat, black puppy we had come for and hauled her into the car. I gave the teenage boy who answered the door a donation and he handed me a baggy of dog food.

When we arrived home and the dog tumbled out onto the grass, my husband said, "That's not a beagle!" Our non-beagle came with worms, mange, and intestinal parasites. Once we gave her lots of care and took out a loan to pay the vet bills, we had a great family dog who even liked the cat.

So mom, dad, four kids, a dog and a cat. Done right?

We were done until I chatted with a neighbor one day who rents out a spare room over his garage. He asked me, "Do you know anyone who wants a turtle and two fish?"

He was cleaning up after some tenants moved out and found a plastic food storage container full of black water. As he started to dump it out, he saw movement. In this oversized bowl were two goldfish and a painted turtle -- alive. He'd been feeding them for six months but didn't really want the pets.

So I brought them home. I was a big hit with the kids for providing surprise pets that hadn't required begging and fourteen family meetings. The boys named the turtle (inexplicably) Zebra. The fish were dubbed (also inexplicably) Bubbles and Pengwi.

My husband came home, examined the newest members of the family, and pronounced, "They can't live in that bowl. They have no room."

"But they like it," I said. "They're used to it."

He shook his head and left for the pet store. He came back with several hundred dollars' worth of aquarium equipment for our formerly free, orphan pets. Apparently, he was now an expert on fish and amphibians.

"These fish can't live with this turtle. Turtles eat goldfish."

"Really?" I said. "He hasn't eaten them yet."

"Just wait. That's what the guy in the pet store said. He said they can live together for months, then one day – BAM!" He eyed the turtle suspiciously, "It's a goldfish slaughterhouse. They need separate environments."

The turtle got his own tank with water and rocks to climb on, a heating lamp, and a fake palm tree. The fish moved into a watery world of blue pebbles, with a decorative castle to swim around, coral pieces, air and water filters.

So the turtle did not eat the goldfish but the cat has a new favorite place to sit and watch our new additions. The dog hasn't really noticed.

KIDS (AND LIZARDS) RETURN TO SCHOOL, MOMS COLLAPSE

You know it's September when your lizard leaves. In our house, Spike, the fifth-grade classroom pet — who spent August with our family — looked at me with his separately moving eyes, grabbed a big cricket with his tongue, and went back to standing completely still for the next four hours. I know it was his way of saying goodbye.

It was a good (if slightly reptilian) summer, but now it was time for the back-to-school rituals performed since our Teenage Daughter began preschool 12 years ago. I should be good at this by now but the first week of September is never without its hectic, gray-hair-inducing calamities.

Our Teenage Daughter is off to high school, commuting every morning with other suburban kids into the city. Meanwhile, the Toddler started kindergarten, (I think I'll be the oldest mom in the class). His brother, the Tween, returns to middle school while our Teenage Son goes to the local public high school. So it's four kids in four different schools, four sets of emergency cards, four schedules, four sets of after-school activities, and four times the opportunity for four hundred and eleven things to go wrong every morning.

I was actually pretty organized this year. I'd ordered school uniforms for my Teenage Daughter, argued over hemlines ("Mom! Why don't you just make me wear a burqa?"), and filled out most of the required forms. My sons, in public school, had enough cargo pants and Mets T-shirts to see them through the year (no fashion arguments there). I'd purchased school supplies that ranged from Transformers lunchboxes to graphing calculators.

So while I dread mornings, evenings are a time to get organized, thwart some of potential morning glitches ("lay out your clothes!" "pack your lunch!"), and generally brace for the first day of school.

Unfortunately, on the eve of school, our Teenage Daughter went into the city to meet some new classmates for tea. I don't know what kind of tea parties these Catholic schools throw, but she came out of it with a strained ligament in her ankle and was unable to walk. She was taken by cab to my mom's nearby apartment. There, the foot was iced, the teenaged girl attached to it fed and cared for.

Meanwhile, at home I had to go to a village meeting, since I am an elected official in our small town -- because I really don't have enough to do. (It's an unpaid volunteer position but at least I get a nice shiny badge.) The Toddler had been running a low fever for a couple of days and I didn't know if he was going to make it to kindergarten the next day. In any case, no parent in their right mind would let their teen babysit in a possibly germy house the night before school started.

I was home with no babysitter – you'd think the mother of four would plan ahead but I never do. I grabbed the nearest fourteen-year-old boy who, luckily, turned out to be our Teenage Son. "I have to go to a meeting to vote on something. Then I'll turn around and come right back. Can you handle watching cartoons with your brother?"

He thought about it. He's a thoughtful chap. "Okay, mom," he said.

I looked at the Tween. "Your older brother is in charge," I told him. "If you fight while I am out, I will kill you." He gave me a thumbs-up and a grin.

I ran upstairs and threw on a suit. I called across the street to the neighbors and told them to watch my house for smoke, power-tool usage, or escaped pets.

I jumped in the car and raced in just as the meeting started. I voted, handed the mayor a note, smiled apologetically, and fled.

I was home 14 minutes after I left.

The next day, ankles were better, fevers had subsided, buses departed. I poured a cup of coffee and took a page out of Spike the Lizard's book – I stood perfectly still for a few minutes enjoying the Zen effect. Lizards have a very long life span. What do they know from back-to-school?

RUN IT UP THE FLAG POLE AND SEE WHO SALUTES

How many relatives does it take to knock down a flag pole?

Two if they are carrying a couch.

A year after we lost my dad, we were selling his house. He'd lived there for thirty years. My kids visited their grandpa there at the beach all their lives, so it was hard to say goodbye to the house.

My sister, my husband, our Teenage Son, and I were out at the house – starting the process of going through my father's stuff. Like the leather couch in the den. It came with the house. I guess Dad thought that a den needed a leather couch and there was a perfectly good one sitting there so he bought it from the previous owners. "After all, these things last forever."

Well, kind of. Thirty years later, you could still sit on it, but it was a sad sight -- cracked and bandaged with electrical tape.

My sister and I were getting overwhelmed, so we ducked out to go for a drive and clear our heads. We left the men – my husband and our Teenage Son – in charge for half an hour. My husband decided, with the girls out of the way, this would be the right time to tackle the big, manly jobs. Like moving the leather couch into the garage. So he went to work, giving our Teenage Son a lesson in the proper way to move heavy furniture.

"Now remember, lift with your knees, not your back. Work with the angles, not against them. See, if you tilt the couch clockwise, not your clockwise – my clockwise…"

There were two routes from the den to the garage. One involved a skinny hallway. The men chose the "out the kitchen door, around to the side of the house" route -- past the flag-pole where our dad, a veteran, flew the American flag and the Marine Corps flag every day. After he died, whenever we would visit the house, my sister would raise the flags in his memory.

The details of what happened next are sketchy. Once the couch was out the kitchen door, rather than lift and carry it, apparently the unorthodox method of flipping the couch end-to-end was adopted.

"See son, this way you let gravity do the job for you –"

Employing strategic thinking, geometric logic, and precision maneuvering – my husband shoved the couch right into the flagpole. The flagpole shuddered from the force only a huge, old leather couch can bring.

The pole shook up and down its length, vibrating wildly, the gold ball on the very top of the pole popped off like a champagne cork, taking the rigging and flags with it. My son and husband stood below, draped in the flags. Very patriotic – literally wrapped in the flag.

My sister and I returned. My sharp-eyed sister saw immediately that something was amiss. "Um – what happened to the flags? Why aren't the flags flying? Who took down Daddy's flags?"

My husband held out the golden ball with a penitent look on his face. "I'm really sorry," he said.

Her mouth opened but no sound came out. Like the guy in Edward Munch's "The Scream." She fled. My husband looked at me and shrugged. He didn't know what to do. I patted his guilty shoulder. I didn't know what to say. Our son looked at both of us with the bemused, exasperated look that teenagers get when they see their parents do something dumb.

My sister came back. "I'm fine now." She didn't look fine.

"Um...we sort of hit it with the couch," my husband helpfully explained.

"The leather couch? Where is it now?"

"In the garage."

"The garage? I see."

My sister, suffice it to say, was not a happy camper. That couch and that flagpole and those flags all symbolized our father to her. Now the flagpole was busted, the flags were folded, and the couch was in the garage.

Change isn't easy. Sometimes it's slow and gradual. And sometimes it's a big, beat-up leather couch crashing into a flagpole.

CAN I BORROW YOUR NANNY?

When we lived in the city, I knew a lot of working moms who hired nannies to watch their kids. I never had a nanny.

Now that I have four kids and live in the suburbs, we don't travel in too many nanny circles. The majority of child watching is done by us, the parents.

But when the kids were all still pretty young and the Toddler was still a baby, my friend Julia hired a nanny for the summer. The Uber Nanny was great with Julia's girls and often took our daughter along to swim at the town lake or stroll the mall.

So when our annual week at the beach arrived, a week when Julia and I took all the kids to my dad's house at the beach to eat Cheese Doodles and lie around on rubber rafts, the Uber Nanny came along. She was prepared to watch not just my friend's two darling girls and our well-behaved daughter, but our three sons as well — including our busy (if not terrible) two-year-old baby!

It took a couple of days before I grew comfortable enough to relinquish control to this efficient young woman, but, after that, no problem. The Uber Nanny had a schedule; she had a plan. She chased the baby around on the beach and splashed with him at water's edge. Then she said, "He's done. I'm taking him home, bathing him, giving him lunch and putting him down for his nap."

It was amazing. The older kids stayed with us swimming and building sand castles until we brought them back to the house where the Uber Nanny told them to change out of their wet things, not leave beach towels on the floor, and not track sand through the house. She told them to clean up the games they played, and to eat snacks only at the kitchen table, instead of crumbing up the entire house.

She made the baby say please or no thank you, and had him choose: in or out, drink juice or play, read a story or color.

At one point, the Uber Nanny told our seven-year-old to shape up or face the longest time out of his life. We never found out what that meant because he shaped up fast.

She asked the kids to set the table, and to chew their food, and to wait a half hour before swimming — and they did. She also said they would need to decide what show they'd watch together without fighting.

A movie was picked, the den was filled with pillows, lights dimmed, popcorn doled out. Parents were banished to dinner in a restaurant together without children. We hardly knew how to react.

The Uber Nanny was fun, but firm. The children took her at face value. There was never a moment of back talk or whining.

Our blissful week ended but I tried to incorporate some of the Uber Nanny's approaches, raised my expectations of the kids a bit, demanded respect, and reminded them to use their manners.

I didn't get the same kind of reaction. What was I doing wrong? Might be that I was related to them. They'd seen too much of me. The Uber Nanny brought a certain mystery... where did she live? What did she do on her day off? How'd she get so "Uber"?

I might be a mom, but the Uber Nanny really knew how to raise children.

A SWEET GOODBYE

When my cousins lost their grandfather, I drove to the town where he had lived to represent my side of the family at the wake. At the last minute, out of necessity, I brought my Toddler along. I thought he might cheer things up.

I was a little nervous since my son had never attended an open casket wake. He entered the big room at the funeral home without hesitation and greeted relatives he hardly knew with hugs and stories about school and his pets and favorite cartoons.

After trying most of the chairs in the room and checking out the flowers, he zeroed in on the coffin at the front of the room. He approached with reverence, knowing that it was not a place to gallop about.

He studied the man lying there and then looked at the framed photo of a young Army officer from the World War II era. He came over to where I stood with my cousins.

"There's a grandpa in the box," he said.

"Yes."

"He died."

"Yes," I said.

"He was a soldier."

"Right, honey."

My son went back to chatting with the older mourners sitting up front. A young woman came in and went over to the casket. She stood there a long time with a very sad expression and seemed to be talking. At one point, it looked as if she put something in the coffin.

Finally she left with a small wave to the family. My cousins told me that she had been their grandfather's health care aide for a long time and that she had become very attached to him.

We said our goodbyes and I turned to call the Toddler. But he was already on his way over happily swinging a large bag of lollipops. "Where did you get that candy?" I asked, assuming one of the relatives had brought it to keep energetic children in line.

"From the box!" he said, delightedly pointing at the coffin.

My cousins were wide-eyed. Those lollipops had been the old man's favorite in his waning years and the young health aide wanted to send him off with a good supply for eternity.

Those candies never made it to eternity. They were stolen from the casket by my Toddler. The kid was half a step away from grave robbing!

I didn't know what to do. "Should we put them back?" I asked.

They were nice about it. "It's okay. It's probably not sanitary for him to be buried with food anyway." Meanwhile, my son was protesting my confiscating his found treasure. "He can have them," one of my cousins offered, not helping the situation at all.

"All right," I said, trying to quell the controversy. "Maybe later," I said (which in our house almost always means "no"). I stashed them reluctantly in my bag and hastened for the door. On the way home, I realized my sleeping child was not traumatized by an open casket funeral. We would, however, need to review the "Look, pray, mourn -- but don't touch" rule before the next occasion.

A DECADE TO REMEMBER

I'm about to turn 49 and I lie in bed whining. I'm looking back, and I'm asking the question, what the hell just
happened?

I started my twenties as a student, became a reporter and
editor, went to grad school twice, and got married – all before
29. There was very little slowing down to mull things over.

I was pregnant at 31, 33, and 36. I had the babies from
those pregnancies at 32, 34, and 37, which means I had an in-
fant in and around the house when I was 33, 35, and 38. It was
kind of a busy decade and, with all that pregnancy (and result-
ing babies), there was clearly no time to pause and reflect. Not
even a pregnant pause.

When I was 41, things slowed down, at least for a year. We
thought we were done. But apparently we were wrong-- our
fourth child was born right before I turned 43.

I had just put our third child on the bus to full day kindergarten when I turned toward the house and felt suddenly quea-
sy. It was an unmistakable sensation. I was 42 and pregnant.
Our youngest son clearly believed it was broadcast-worthy, he

stood on our front porch yelling, "My mom's gonna have a baby!"

That brought the neighbors out.

Motherhood is completely different at 42 than it was at 32. When you're 32 and you have a newborn baby, you are exhausted, cranky, and overwhelmed. But when you are 42... actually, it's the same but now you're 10 years older!

These last five years have flown and, once again, we are putting another child on the bus.

By this time next year, our Teenage Daughter will know where she is going to college. Our Teenage Son will be halfway through high school. Our Tween will have only one more year of middle school. Our Toddler will be a big boy first grader. Our dog turns eight, our cat nine, not sure how old the turtle is, really don't care how old the fish are.

A few days ago, my neighbor Annie called me laughing – she wanted me to know about a show on the Learning Channel. "It's called '70 and Pregnant,'" she said, "and I thought of you!" She thought this was hysterical.

"When can we expect the next one?" she snorted, as she hung up the phone, unable to continue due to the hilarity.

"70 and Pregnant?" I can beat that, Learning Channel! I've been 31, 33, 36, and 42 and pregnant. Do the math! Add it all up and you get "142 and Pregnant!"

WEIGHT LOSS PLAN

I was gaining weight. Slowly, diabolically. It was sneaking up on me. Obviously I was doing something wrong. I can't quite figure it out. The fact that I was eating whatever I wanted and spending half my life sitting in a car operating the Susan Konig Taxi Service for two teenagers, a 'tween and a toddler might have had something to do with it...

And of course my weight gain coincided with my thirtieth high school reunion. Like all women facing their 30th high school reunion I had to either launch an immediate 3-week drastic starvation diet, or invest in industrial-strength Spanx. I decided on a diet. (And Spanx.)

Gone are the good old days of easy, sudden weight loss. When I was in my twenties, I had all kinds of special diets that worked. There was the Bran Muffin, Coffee, and Cigarettes diet. I invented that one myself. It involved eating the occasional bran muffin, drinking a lot of coffee, and smoking a lot of cigarettes (hence the name). I wasn't particularly healthy, and I was a little wired, but I was skinny. Oh, and I had chronic bronchitis – there's an appetite suppressant.

In college, my roommates and I went on the TWA Stewardess Diet. As I recall, it consisted primarily of beets. I don't know why TWA stewardesses were flying around eating nothing but beets, but I tried it. A little problem: I hate beets. So I eliminated beets from the all-beets diet and ended up eating nothing. This worked for about one afternoon. Then I fainted. I promptly went off my all-beets diet and went out for a cheeseburger.

So, this time, I knew I couldn't be trusted to do it all myself. I signed up for a well-known alliterative program that involves going to regular meetings…but the thought of sitting in a meeting with other women talking about my thighs is about as appealing to me as…well, as sitting anywhere talking with anyone about my thighs. Which is to say, not too appealing. Plus, my children are resistant to my going out. So I opted for the doing the program anonymously online.

They've got a "points system." It takes a little getting used to. Every food has a point value and, if you keep to your number of points, over time, you lose weight. The first week I had to borrow points from the following week just to stay alive.

My husband calls the plan Pudge Pounders. I don't mind. Chubby people like him are sarcastic that way.

A few weeks later, I had lost 10 pounds. He asked me to sign him up for the plan's online program for men. "I want to lose 10 pounds," he says, "in a week."

"You can't do that," I say. "It's not healthy. You have to exercise every day and limit ice cream to once a week."

"Can I eat ice cream every day and limit exercise to once a week?"

Pass the beets.

THE 30TH REUNION

I was appointed class captain so I am in charge of gathering as many "girls" as possible from the class of 1980 for our reunion luncheon. I don't know how I ended up as class captain. I received an email from the school alumnae office congratulating me on the honor of being selected as class captain. I wrote back asking how many people had turned it down before they got to me. They sent me a list of my old classmates. We all spent thirteen years in a convent school in New York City wearing the same woolen kilts.

Getting everyone to actually sign up was not as easy as the Alumnae office said it would be. Old friends weren't getting back to me or were non-committal about showing up. Until I got in touch with Judy. Judy was a really fun girl in high school, the life of the party in college, and all-around pretty much the same now. Judy married a Frenchman and lives in France. She is all over Facebook usually photographed wearing a feather boa and holding a champagne bottle at an AC/DC concert.

Her dad was a diplomat and Judy learned from her mom how to entertain and make people comfortable. She says there are usually about 25 people at her house for lunch or dinner every weekend. That's just how she rolls.

I told her I was having some trouble scaring up friends for the reunion. Judy kicked off by announcing on Facebook that she was coming to New York City from Europe, where she's lived for twenty years. She was basically throwing down the gauntlet -- the excuse that traveling to the reunion would be too difficult was not acceptable. A bunch of us Facebookers agreed and formed an online group for what we unofficially called JudyPalooza, and even those who lived out of state as far as California started to think that it sounded like a pretty fun idea.

But that wasn't good enough for Judy. She started asking us about "girls" we hadn't seen since graduation day, women who weren't on the 'Net and hadn't kept in touch with anyone. She managed to track them down like a ruthless detective and badgered them into coming through phone calls and even snail mail. I think the women were shocked to actually get a letter from an old friend or pick up their home phones to hear her familiar laughing voice. She told them, "Well, I'm coming in from France during a general strike and an oil embargo so maybe you could get your butt in a cab for 40 blocks." It worked.

We picked a beautiful waterfront restaurant and a lovely day. Meeting friends for a nice brunch in a conveniently located restaurant is a lot easier than physically going back to your old school. After all, there might be some stern and extremely elderly nun roaming the halls, waiting to remind you of some shortcoming you had in 1978. I guess we were right about the location since about half our class agreed to come. The last in-school reunion, only about 5 girls had showed up.

I picked out something slimming to wear, covered the gray hair, and got my nails done.

Most of us arrived feeling a little nervous but soon realized that, after thirty years, we were all still recognizable. We treated each other as if we were still in high school. We fell into the old camaraderie, screaming as each new person arrived, giggling and guffawing a lot, much to the annoyance of everyone else in the restaurant. They had clearly picked the wrong place.

We remembered the time we were bussed to a dance at a boys' boarding school, called the Abbey and, afterwards, the monks locked us in the infirmary for the night to keep everyone chaste. We passed around our yearbook and speculated on the whereabouts of the other half of the class. The old photos had somehow gotten much smaller since we all had to hold them at arms' length to see them.

We caught up on how far 30 years has taken us.

Shannon, who I thought was destined for Broadway, is married to a sheriff in rural Florida. Her town is so small that a typical greeting in the local grocery store is, "Hey, your husband arrested my husband last night." Jennifer got her PhD in psychology and helps the neglected and abused. Sue has triplets and Liz has twins. Carina's a travel agent, Cathy C. took to the stage, and Cathy P. advocates for shelter pets. There are a couple of lawyers, a polo player, and an animal communicator. Like Dr. Doolittle, she talks to the animals. But do they talk back?

When the check came, Liz, the class president, assumed her old organizational role divvying up the check 18 ways.

After about three hours, we left, reluctantly. The maître d' sighed with relief. JudyPalooza was a success and we promised to try to meet again, same time, next year.

EPILOGUE: THE NOBLE EXPERIMENT

God bless the children but sometimes a Mom needs to get away. And I don't mean to the local Starbucks for an hour. I waited 'til summer, negotiated the terms with my understanding husband, and finagled a whole week at a writer's retreat in Vermont.

After driving a mere 330 miles, singing all the way, I found myself clomping through the deep woods of Vermont on an August morning and pondering my role as a mom, a writer, and a citizen of Earth.

I was attempting to spend a week writing at a remote cabin in the woods, three states away from home without cell phone service, Internet, kids, laundry, running water, mortgage payments, or husbands.

There's not a lot to do in a cabin. I found myself looking for stuff to do. I went outside and did a yoga pose because I could. Mountain pose. You stand there like a mountain. Breathe. Ah. Okay, that killed a couple of minutes. I went back inside. I made a scarf into a throw for the sofa, stuck up pictures the kids drew with push pins, organized the five items on my desk, changed my screensaver to a photo of the kids at the beach, put on two layers of Sally Hansen nail strengthener, and took a nap.

I wished I had a broom because I wanted to sweep. I never clean at home. I guess I don't have the time. I wanted my little cabin to be spit spot. How can a writer write in a dusty cabin?

I didn't miss cleaning my house. I missed my kids. I know a lot of moms who have been away from their kids for a week but not me. I am always home. I felt like a runaway. I didn't miss the fighting and the dirty socks on the floor and the toothpaste explosions in the bathroom and children saying yes they brushed their teeth when they didn't...or the dog barking six million times to be let out or be let in and everyone pretending they don't hear her even though they are sitting right there!

Or waking up to the garbage truck which came early and we forgot to put out the trash and there's kitty litter and old meat in there and now we have to keep it another week even though I went through the agony of birth three times to have three sons who can take out the garbage not to mention their father and why should I have to!?

And when I finally drive down to the main road where the cell connection kicks in to call home and hear that everything is fine, I feel guilty.

My Toddler asks if I am driving home yet and it is only the first day. He is being a trouper about it and wants me to take him for pizza and juice when I come home. I tell him I have a picture up on the wall that he drew of us walking the dog. The dog hangs from a string in my hand like a yoyo and his eyes seems to be popping a bit -- like big fried eggs.

One night, I'm walking back from the distant outhouse that has defined my retreat – it's down a hacked out path through the tall grass, no lights. When will I go to the bathroom? I ask myself several times a day. I miss my kids, yes, but I miss indoor plumbing almost as much.

I wonder: Should I drink that Diet Coke stored in my cooler -- is it worth a trip to the bathroom in the dark? I'm a city girl and these dark woods are scary. I decide to brush my teeth from a water bottle, skip the Diet Coke, and go to bed.

After a day or two I find my courage, I know the trail now and have a good flashlight. The biggest threat the woods have to offer is mosquitoes – or so I think…

Lunch is left on a stump in a picnic basket around noon. So the only time I see anyone is for dinner in the house where Chris, the retreat owner, cooks and serves food on the porch. We talk about writing. There are supposed to be a bunch of other writers but business is slow. Or maybe the other writers have been eaten by mosquitoes. So I am alone with my host half the time. The other half, his little 3-year old daughter is there and adorable, which makes me miss my kids even more.

I discover that my host is a Sasquatch researcher. I've known him for years (he taught me in grad school) and now he has this beautiful retreat for writers, but I didn't know he was a Sasquatch researcher.

"Oh that's interesting," I say over dinner.

"I just wrote a book about Sasquatches. I'm not an expert," he says humbly. But he has done little else except track Sasquatches for two years. "I will tell you about it on the last day because you may get freaked out and want to leave," he says with a melancholy smile.

I don't believe in Sasquatch. But if I did, I'd be comforted knowing they're far away from Vermont, I think, or in the Northwest parts of the US or maybe in Kentucky. Right?

No, I am wrong.

"They're here in Vermont. About 18 miles away."

Oh. And with those big feet, they can be here in no time.

He tells me about sightings. He is not overly anxious to share all this which makes me feel better. Chris doesn't look like the Unabomber. He wears polar fleeces and sandals. He has interviewed lots of credible people who were not looking for Sasquatches but, apparently, came across them in the woods.

Sasquatches are like people, says Chris. Those who have encountered them say it is like looking into a person's eyes, not an animal. They are like another species of human. One group he researches lives by a dumpster behind a Wal-Mart. How did I not hear about this?

Chris tells me about the Sasquatch knocking habits. "They knock on trees and answer each other that way to locate each other." It may be a hunting technique to corral deer and trap them.

"Then how are they prepared?" I ask, wondering how this peaceful shy critter eats.

"There have been stacks of deer found with their hearts and livers ripped out." Hmm. I'm hoping they would have no interest in my internal organs.

The next day I take a walk on a trail near the retreat. Every little stick pile or bent sapling says Sasquatch to me. I think of the little stuffed cat that Chris has placed in a basket nailed to a tree. I thought it was a game for his little daughter. But it is at Sasquatch eye level, about 6 feet up. There are piles of rocks on stumps, offerings or gifts which supposedly Sasquatches take and replace with other gifts, like shiny stones or circles of feathers. Sometimes they shriek like other creatures to communicate. Why do I suddenly know so much about Bigfoot?

The rest of the time I try to work and sleep. I am in the A frame which is adorable and I love it. But under the roof at night, once I've convinced myself that the Sasquatch won't come in my locked door (a screen door with a tiny hook closure), and clamber up the ladder to my sleeping loft, I look out the skylights at the stars and the tops of the pine trees. Then the owls start. I mean a really loud freakin' owl. "HOOOOOOT! Hoo Hooo HOOOOOOOOT!"

Then the answer comes from the friend owl: "WHOO OOOOOOO! Whoooooo, Whoooooo, WHOOOOOOOOO OOOOO!"

This goes on for about 20 minutes. Then I fall asleep. Then the rattle of the aluminum roof wakes me with a start. Something is on the roof. But it's an A frame. It would have to be a remarkably agile Sasquatch to walk on a sharply pitched roofline like that. The window by my head looks right up at the peak of the roofline. The stars make it bright outside (something I never knew they could do) but there are no other lights or major cities near here.

Then I see. It's bats! They are flying in right at the peak and crawling between the aluminum and the wood frame of the house. I hear their little scritchy footsteps as they kind of galumph around up there. They come and go like flight attendants sharing an apartment. One flies in, another takes off. It's like an aircraft carrier, only noisier.

This was more like having really annoying upstairs neighbors that make you mutter, "Oh for gods' sakes!" And put a pillow over your head.

The bats are incredible graceful when they take off and actually make a swooshing sound like something being sucked through a pneumatic tube (look it up on Google, kids).

I ask Chris the next day about the owls. "You didn't hear?" I say. "They were so loud."

"Oh, I had the AC on…but it was probably Sasquatches calling to each other…."

During our next dinner conversation, it sounds to me like Chris is searching for meaning, or for God. He says,

"Sasquatches either exist and we have to deal with that and find a way to approach it, or they don't. If they exist, we need information, a way to accept this information that will be a tipping point for people when it happens."

All this sounds like a preparation for some kind of spiritual revelation. He recently split with the mom of his little girl. I wonder if he is questioning all of life and using Sasquatch as the central meaning, the Godot he is waiting for.

I leave Chris for the dark path back to my cabin and wish I was having dinner with my husband.

I miss him and the kids. Sure, the mosquitoes, bats, and Sasquatch are an interesting change of pace, but...

This is a particularly artificial retreat even though I am in the land of organic everything and free trade hemp soap. Life isn't really like this. My life isn't like this. I don't live with a handful of things: five shirts, two pairs of shoes, a washcloth, and four photos of my kids. I have a bunch of stuff. I don't spend much time at home wondering about Sasquatch tree-bending habits.

At the retreat, I found time. I mean I literally rediscovered it. I used to fantasize about all the time I had in my early twenties. The days seemed hundreds of hours long. I would lie on my futon writing page after page in my journal about some lame boyfriend or how I wanted to be a writer but didn't know if I could give myself permission and blah blah blah.

I often wondered how that time just disappeared. Well, it didn't. It's in a cabin in East Calais, Vermont. Just sitting there. Almost instantly, I went from being a wife and mother of four and, just by driving 330 miles away, I have time. Tons of time. Like I look at the clock and only 10 minutes has passed.

At home, my morning falls into a vortex and the school bus is back at the corner and the day is gone.

So it's the kids. Very time consuming people.

And yet, I could make time for myself. I could go somewhere to write and treat it as a retreat or a real workday like a person has in an office and know that I can't get the missing lunch to school, or I shouldn't do the grocery shopping although this is the optimal time, and if I don't get the laundry going and the bills paid it will be another day behind....

Still I'm not getting any writing done. I miss my family (and my indoor plumbing). So this experiment is not working. I cannot live without my kids though apparently they can live without me. "Daddy bought the 24 pack of hot dogs," my Teenage Son explains during one side of the road phone call.

I am supposed to be writing a mystery series for kids. I am writing about missing my kids and being alone in the woods with a Sasquatch enthusiast. Who, by the way, was struggling with his own writing because of the laundry and the shopping and the house and his little girl. He would probably get more done if he went to my house. So it wasn't the solitude of a writer's cabin 330 miles from home, maybe it was about getting away from one's laundry.

On the last day, I drive down to town and go to the drug store. I decide to buy my Toddler the biggest toy in the store. I have already gotten the older kids "I ♥ Vermont" shirts and moose-y snow globes. But he needs to know that mom really loves him and missed him. Then I see it. A giant SpongeBob doll that is about 48 inches high. I strap him into my passenger seat and begin the drive home. Toll takers smile and a passing school bus of kids returning from day camp peer out their windows pointing. Look at the lady driving with the giant SpongeBob doll! I wonder what they think...

How could they know I am a mom who just survived a week in the woods dodging Sasquatch and is racing home to her husband and kids?

CPSIA information can be obtained at www.ICGtesting.com
Printed in the USA
LVOW11s0250280415

436351LV00001B/47/P